History of the Mosaic Templars of America

History of the Mosaic Templars of America

Its Founders and Officials

EDITED BY
A. E. BUSH AND P. L. DORMAN

INTRODUCTION BY
JOHN WILLIAM GRAVES

The University of Arkansas Press
Fayetteville
2008

Originally printed by Little Rock Central Printing Company,
copyright 1924 by A. E. Bush and P. L. Dorman

Special thanks to the Department of Arkansas Heritage,
the Mosaic Templars Cultural Center, and the Black
History Commission of Arkansas, whose generous
support made this publication possible.

ISBN-10: 1-55728-882-8
ISBN-13: 978-1-55728-882-0

12   11   10   09   08   5   4   3   2   1

CONTENTS

INTRODUCTION
John William Graves

A casual happenstance led to the founding of the Mosaic Templars of America in 1882, an organization destined to become at its height one of the largest black business enterprises in the United States. A young black resident of Little Rock, Arkansas, John E. Bush, and a white acquaintance were standing on a Little Rock street corner passing the time of day when an aged black woman approached and requested a donation to assist in burying her deceased husband. Both men contributed, but as the woman turned and left "the white man, prefacing his remarks with an oath, said, 'I cannot see or understand your race. When they work they throw their earnings away and whenever a Negro dies or needs help the public must be worried to death by beggars—it is a shame!'" (Except when otherwise identified, all quotations in this introduction are derived from *The Mosaic Templars of America—Its Founders and Officials.*)

Insensitive and offensive as the remark was, Bush was nonetheless moved to action by it. He and a close friend and fellow employee in the U.S. Railway Mail Service, Chester W. Keatts, proceeded to launch the Mosaic Templars society, whose central purpose from the beginning was to provide burial and life insurance for its members. Joining with thirteen other persons, they organized Zephro Temple Number 1 on May 21, 1882. Pooling their funds, they rented a building and began placing advertisements and announcements in the press in order to solicit membership applications. Applications came in not only from Little Rock but from De Vall's Bluff, Prescott, Sweet Home, and several other Arkansas towns. Soon, enough money had been collected from dues to allow the group to incorporate by the spring of the following year, and on May 24, 1883, the Templars received an official charter from the State of Arkansas.

The charter bestowed upon the Mosaic Templars of America was granted under an 1875 Arkansas statute that authorized the incorporation of benevolent associations, and like many such associations of that day and time, the Mosaic Templars organization operated as a traditional fraternal order. New applicants were inducted into the group through the conferring of eight secret initiation degrees administered through its local temples. For a very brief period, both men and women met together in the first temple, Zephro Temple Number 1. However, "It was discovered that in accordance with the few existing laws that governed them, they could not easily expand their operations unless separate branches were organized for both men and women." Apparently for this reason, separate lodges known as "Chambers" were begun for female Mosaics. The chambers had their own rituals and distinct initiation rites and also exercised supervision over separate chapters for Mosaic youth known as "Palaces." The very first of the chambers, Lone Star Chamber Number 1, was formally instituted in Little Rock on August 2, 1883.

The name of the order was derived from the Biblical prophet Moses, who had delivered the Children of Israel from slavery in Pharoah's Egypt and led them to eventual freedom and prosperity

in a new Promised Land. The rituals and ceremonies of the Mosaic Templars were based upon
this story of deliverance, and they must have been
especially moving and poignant for the group's
early members; since it was begun only seventeen
years after the ending of slavery in the United
States, for most of them the experience of bondage
would still have been a vivid memory.

No doubt the fraternal aspects of the Mosaic
Templars of America contributed greatly to the
organization's rapid expansion and growth. Within
the temples, chambers, and palaces, members
could carve out autonomous spaces for themselves
where they could develop their own social outlets,
leadership capacities, and also obtain a respite and
haven from painful encounters with white prejudice and condescension. Equally important to the
order's success, however, was the leadership provided by its founders, Chester W. Keatts and
John E. Bush. Both were still young men in their
twenties at the dawning of the organization, possessed of energy and ambition. They were also
early beneficiaries of the new Reconstruction–era
school system established in Little Rock and sur-

rounding Pulaski County, where both of them had obtained good educations and where Bush had served for a time as principal of Little Rock's Capitol Hill public school. From the inception of the Mosaic Templars until his death in 1908, Keatts served as the group's Grand Mosaic Master; simultaneously, until his own death in 1916, John E. Bush held the post of Grand Scribe and headed the Endowment Department that administered its insurance program, the heart of the Templars' enterprise. Their zeal and competence and the close working relationship that they developed and maintained provided needed stability during the Mosaic Templars crucial formative years.

As the Mosaic Templars steadily expanded and grew and new chapters were added throughout Arkansas, the need developed for a more formal organizational structure. The Templars' 1883 Charter of Incorporation gave the group the power "to make its own constitution, laws, discipline and general laws for the government of the entire order in America," and a constitution was drafted which was approved and took effect on September 9, 1886. It stated the general purposes of the order and identified its classes of insurance policies and specified how policyholders would be paid. The constitution also created an extensive management system headed by the Grand Mosaic Master, who functioned as the order's chief executive, exercising general oversight authority over the national organization and its various local temples. He or his designee was charged with visiting each subordinate temple once a year, and he could suspend any subordinate temple when he determined that it was "failing to comply with the Constitution and Grand Laws of the Order." He also exercised similar authority over the women's units. Article VI of the constitution stated, "The Lady Chambers and Palaces of this Order shall be governed by the Constitution, laws, etc., as other Temples, and shall be under the special watch-care and guardianship of the Grand Mosaic Master."

The order's second most important official was the Grand Scribe, who was charged with keeping official records and conducting correspondence and, most significantly, performing the chief functions regarding claims and disbursement of insurance payments to policyholders.

Other national officers were a Grand Aaronic
Master, who functioned as a vice-president; a
Grand Treasurer; and a Chief Grand Deputy, who
functioned as the order's auditor and also performed the duties of the Grand Mosaic Master
and Grand Aaronic Master in their absences.
Finally, the constitution also established the
offices of Grand Chaplain, Grand Marshal,
Grand Warden, and Grand Inside and Outside
Guardians. All of the above officials were to serve
"for the period of one year, or until their successors are elected and qualified," save for the Grand
Mosaic Master and the Grand Scribe, who were
to "serve until all policies taken under them shall
have matured and been paid," a provision that
guaranteed the equivalent of a life appointment
for each of the founders.

Five of the above officers—the Grand Mosaic
Master, the Grand Scribe, the Grand Aaronic
Master, the Grand Treasurer, and the Chief Grand
Deputy—served as permanent members of a
Grand Committee of Management, which also
included four additional members elected at gen-
eral meetings of the organization referred to as ses-
sions of the Supreme Grand Temple or National

Grand Lodge. The constitution described the Grand Committee of Management as "the Grand Head of this organization" and bestowed upon it the same authority to transact general business and institute acts and orders as was possessed by the Supreme Grand Temple itself.

Further elaboration of this management system occurred in 1905 when the National Grand Lodge meeting in Memphis, Tennessee, adopted a resolution permitting any state with seven or more active temples or chambers in good financial standing to organize a State Grand Temple. The granting of charters and the administration of the order's insurance program remained under control of the national office in Little Rock, but the new State Grand Temples or Lodges could assist in membership recruitment and could if they wished provide an additional death benefit to members beyond that specified in insurance policies, the latter to be financed by a special state dues assessment or tax.

It is worth noting that the State Grand Temples appear to have enhanced the role of women within the order. It became an unwritten rule that the position of State Grand Scribe would be held by a female Mosaic, and in 1910 Mrs. C. C. Bell of Little Rock was elected State Aaronic Mistress of Arkansas, "the only woman ever attaining this rank in the order." The augmented role of women in the state groups may in turn have influenced the practices of the National Grand Temple; by the 1920s several women simultaneously were serving on the national Committee of Management.

Along with its increase in numbers, the Mosaic Templars expanded in regard to its programs and activities. From 1884 to 1895 it operated the Mosaic National Building and Loan Association (MNBLA). Designed to provide capital at reasonable rates of interest to Templars members adjudged to be good credit risks, the MNBLA provided them with loans for the purchase of homes, mortgage relief for existing loans from other financial institutions, and commercial and personal loans for a multiplicity of purposes. Since blacks often found it difficult to obtain lines of credit and access to capital through white-owned banks and institutions, the MNBLA helped fill a vital community need.

Among other ventures undertaken by the Templars were publication of a national newspaper, the *Mosaic Guide,* beginning in 1885, and operation of a medical department, commencing in 1908. Initially the chief function of the medical department was to sponsor scientific lectures upon health and hygiene for members of the Templars. At the National Grand Lodge meeting held in Little Rock, Arkansas, in 1917, however, a resolution was adopted authorizing the erection of a Mosaic Templars general hospital and sanitarium. To many members the need for such an institution was self-evident. When admitted at all to white-owned medical facilities, African Americans found themselves confined to separate, segregated wards and often purportedly received inferior care. An African American physician could not treat his patients in such hospitals without having first obtained a white "associate," who had to sign all of his medical orders before they could be executed. Even a black physician with a degree from the Harvard Medical School, such as Little Rock's early twentieth-century physician Dr. G. W. S. Ish, had to submit to this humiliating procedure.

Pursuant to the 1917 resolution, a Mosaic State Hospital began operating, probably beginning in 1919, in an annex building adjacent to the order's national headquarters building in Little Rock. Long-range plans contemplated constructing a much larger national hospital and sanitarium at Hot Springs, Arkansas. Although this facility was never built, a site for it was acquired when seven acres of land in downtown Hot Springs was purchased at a market value of sixty thousand dollars in 1924. Complementing the above effort, the Mosaic Templars order was granted a charter for a nurse training school in 1929, and, according to a description of the hospital issued in 1931, such a training school was still affiliated with it at that time.

One new program was consciously designed to keep Mosaic Templars members out of the hospital. A Uniform Rank Department was created at the National Grand Lodge meeting held at Memphis, Tennessee, in 1905, and "the greater aim of the proponents of this law was for the proper training of our youth in the various forms of calisthenics." Placed under the supervision of a Major General, its various state jurisdictions also taught members the "manual of arms," and in some ways its existence was intended to compensate for the fact that, by the beginning of the twentieth century, African Americans had been effectively excluded from southern state militias. The various drill teams of the Uniform Rank Department became especially popular, and special parades in which they performed appear to have become regular features of the National Grand Lodge meetings. Although the activities of the Uniform Rank Department were particularly appealing to young men, it also maintained a women's auxiliary unit whose members "in their later drill contests proved themselves equal in a great many respects, to the strict discipline of the military."

A final benefit to members of the Mosaic Templars of America was provided by its national Monument Department. Created out of the consolidation of several earlier state monument programs in 1914, the Monument Department collected an annual tax of fifty cents from each Mosaic Templar and provided each deceased member with "a well-designed uniform Vermont marble marker, with suitable inscription." Hundreds of these markers with their Mosaic Templars iconography can still be found in historic black cemeteries scattered throughout the United States. One such burial place is the historic Fraternal Cemetery in Little Rock, Arkansas, where both of the cofounders of the Mosaic Templars of America were laid to rest and where many of its other early officers and members are interred.

All of the above activities and initiatives made the Mosaic Templars organization even more appealing to prospective recruits. Of the two founders, Chester W. Keatts died on January 16, 1908. At his death the organization already had grown from its original fifteen members in 1882 to some eleven thousand members; its assets now totaled approximately twenty thousand dollars, and the order had spread from Arkansas to seven additional states.

Keatts's successor as Grand Mosaic Master was William Alexander, originally from Mississippi, who built further on these advances. Aided by a young, energetic associate, John Hamilton

McConico, "He and Mr. Alexander made a modern Paul and Silas combination, and with their fiery eloquence and untiring zeal, literally set the woods on fire with Mosaic enthusiasm, shooting conviction right into the hearts of all who would give them an audience and the Mosaics became the fastest growing fraternal organization in the race."

Alexander's efforts were cut short when he was murdered by a disgruntled employee in Frankfort, Kentucky, on November 1, 1913. Vigorous membership campaigns were continued, however, under the next Grand Mosaic Master, the Reverend S. J. Elliott, a minister of the Colored Methodist Episcopal Church from Alabama. By the time of the death of cofounder John E. Bush on December 11, 1916, the Mosaic Templars of America boasted eighty thousand dues-paying members belonging to some two thousand chapters located in twenty-six states, Central and South America, the Canal Zone, and the West Indies. The grand total of net assets possessed by the national organization and its state affiliates was $309,293.78.

By 1913 the Mosaic Templars of America organization had become large and prosperous enough to erect a new headquarters building or National Mosaic Temple at the southwest corner of Broadway and West Ninth streets in downtown Little Rock. Anchoring the east end of Little Rock's West Ninth Street black business district, the Mosaic Templars headquarters building was at the time of its construction one of the largest and most imposing buildings in Arkansas's capital. Understandably it was viewed with pride by many contemporary blacks as an outward and visible sign of their race's capacities and potential for advancement. A handsome three-story brick building occupying over half a block, its exterior façade was embellished with restrained neoclassical elements and motifs. The Templars order leased the first floor of the building to various shops and commercial enterprises in order to generate income that would help pay for the building's construction and upkeep. The second floor initially was used to house the Templars' own offices. The third floor contained a beautiful auditorium, flooded with natural light from vertical rows of large windows on its north and south sides. The auditorium was topped with an ornate pressed-tin ceiling, while below was a spacious, open wooden floor. At the west end of the auditorium was a raised platform and stage and a small orchestra pit. At the east end, looking out at the parquet area and stage, was a horseshoe-shaped balcony surrounded by a balustrade crested with a gleaming wooden railing. Beyond the auditorium, farther to the east, a small staircase led to an "Elk's Rest," which in essence functioned as a partial fourth floor.

One of the most attractive interior spaces to be found in any Little Rock commercial building of the time, the auditorium quickly became a vibrant center of African American community life. Held there were not only many Templars' functions but innumerable plays, dances, and concerts featuring a number of legendary jazz and blues artists and performers. In later years it provided a venue for some of Little Rock's early motion picture shows, and it was also the setting for many high-school commencement exercises.

Continued rapid expansion of the Mosaic Templars created a need for additional office space, and a two-story brick annex was constructed immediately to the south of the main headquarters building in 1918 (its second floor

would later house the Mosaic Templars hospital).
A third structure, also a two-story brick edifice,
which housed the offices of the Arkansas state
Mosaic Templars organization, was built immediately to the south of the annex building in 1921.
Henceforth, this triplex of Mosaic Templars
buildings would occupy the land on the west side
of Broadway Street lying between West Ninth and
West Tenth streets.

When the Mosaic Templars headquarters
building was formally dedicated on October 13,
1913, the ceremony was one of Little Rock's major
events of the year. Booker T. Washington traveled
from Tuskegee, Alabama, to deliver the principal
address and was greeted by an assembled crowd
of five thousand persons who thronged outside
the new building. Over two thousand citizens,
including whites as well as blacks, then squeezed
inside the building's third-floor auditorium to
hear Washington, who was officially introduced
and welcomed to the city by Little Rock mayor
Charles E. Taylor.

The selection of Washington to deliver the principal dedicatory address was no accident. Although
the Templars organization had been founded

before Booker T. Washington's own rise to national prominence, it was the very embodiment of Washington's ideal of racial advancement through economic self-help within the American capitalist system. Mosaic Templars' leader John E. Bush was a charter member of Washington's National Negro Business League, serving on its executive committee for many years and for a time as one of its national vice-presidents. Bush lobbied successfully to have the league's national convention held in Little Rock in August 1911, and the Mosaic Templars in turn held their own national meeting at Tuskegee, Alabama, in July 1914. Washington himself purchased a Mosaic Templars insurance policy, and he devoted an entire chapter of his 1907 book *The Negro in Business* to John E. Bush and Little Rock's black business community. One of Bush's biographers, historian C. Calvin Smith, has observed in an article published in the summer 1995 issue of the *Arkansas Historical Quarterly* that, given their similar backgrounds and life experiences, it is not surprising that Bush and Washington became mutual admirers and friends.

Washington was catapulted into national

prominence by the speech that he delivered to the Southern States Cotton Exposition held in Atlanta, Georgia, in 1895. In his famous "Atlanta Compromise" address, Washington appeared to suggest that blacks would eschew active political involvements, at least for the time being, if southern white leaders would support his race's efforts for self-help and economic advancement and especially support the kinds of vocational and industrial training programs that were offered at schools such as his own Tuskegee Institute. His apparent accommodationist racial stance was later criticized by W. E. B. Du Bois and other leaders of the Niagara Movement, who urged African Americans to maintain fealty to the legacy of political activism and protest established by Frederick Douglass and other pioneer black abolitionist and civil rights leaders. The debate between adherents of these differing racial philosophies continued for decades and in some limited measure has persisted to the present day.

Considering his own close association with Washington, it is somewhat paradoxical that Bush evinced a lifelong interest in politics. "I am a politician," he confessed, "first for the interest of my race, secondly because I like it." Like the great majority of African Americans of his era, Bush affiliated with the Republican Party, the party of Lincoln, and it was probably no mere coincidence that his first rise to prominence in local Republican affairs began in the very year in which he cofounded the Mosaic Templars. His leadership role in the rapidly expanding black fraternal and insurance organization soon catapulted him into the front ranks of his race. Local white Republicans began to notice him, and his fellow Mosaics no doubt provided him with a solid base of support among black Republicans. In 1883 he was elected to represent the sixth ward of Pulaski County at the Arkansas Republican state convention, and the following year he was chosen secretary of the state convention. Pulaski County Republicans elected him temporary chairman of their convention in 1892; also in 1892 he and two other African Americans, Mifflin W. Gibbs and William La Porte, won election as Arkansas delegates to the Republican national convention. In 1894 Bush was listed as secretary of the Pulaski County Republican organization.

Bush also partly owed his political success to his close association with Powell Clayton, a former Reconstruction-era governor and United States senator who remained after Reconstruction the dominant figure in Arkansas Republican affairs for the remainder of the nineteenth century. After Bush helped thwart an opposition movement against Clayton in the 1880s spearheaded by some dissident blacks, the grateful and much relieved white leader offered him a monetary reward for his support. When Bush declined the offer, Clayton asked what he wished, instead. Bush replied, "Your influence as long as you have any and as long as I deserve it." "You have it," Clayton responded.

Clayton valued personal loyalty and fidelity to the Republican Party's chain of command more than any other quality, and he proved true to his word, joining Bush and other African Americans in keeping "lily-white" movements at bay within state Republican ranks. Under their tacit understanding, African Americans supported Clayton's primacy and in turn were assured a subordinate yet important voice in the Arkansas Republican Party. Bush himself, with Clayton's backing, was appointed receiver of the United States Land

Office in Little Rock by President William McKinley in 1898.

That Bush incidentally performed well in this important post is suggested by the circumstances surrounding his reappointment in 1902. Bush faced opposition in his bid for reappointment, and politics never made stranger bedfellows than in the coalition formed against the Mosaic Templars leader: it consisted of local lily-white elements among Arkansas Republicans and Boston, Massachusetts, Negroes who distrusted his close friendship with Booker T. Washington. In his successful fight to retain his office, Bush secured endorsements from Washington and Powell Clayton and from Little Rock's white business establishment. Little Rock's mayor, board of trade, bar association, every bank in the city, and "business houses without exception" all forwarded letters of recommendation to President Theodore Roosevelt. With this backing from Little Rock whites, Bush won his fight for reappointment and continued to hold his position for eleven more years, until a Democrat, Woodrow Wilson, became President in 1913.

* * *

By the time of Bush's reappointment in 1901, however, the parameters of opportunity had already begun to narrow for African Americans in Arkansas. As early as the late 1880s and early 1890s, hard times in southern agriculture and tumbling cotton prices and incomes had caused thousands of white farmers to abandon the Democratic Party and join third-party agrarian insurgencies such as the Union Labor and Populist movements. Alarmed Democrats responded by "playing the race card" in order to distract attention from troublesome economic issues that were beginning to divide the white vote. To hammer home the point that the Democratic Party was the party of white supremacy, Democratic lawmakers began to enact a new series of Jim Crow segregation laws mandating physical separation of races. While a variety of arguments were advanced in favor of the new segregation measures, their greatest appeal to many whites stemmed from the fact that they restored to them the full racial exclusiveness they craved. As contemporary parlance phrased it, such measures served to "keep the Negro in his place."

Because of his prominence in both the Mosaic Templars society and in the Arkansas Republican Party, by the 1890s John E. Bush had clearly established himself as one of the two or three most important African American civic and political leaders in Arkansas. He was ideally positioned to rally black opposition to the new series of Jim Crow segregation laws being proposed by white Democratic legislators during this watershed period in southern and Arkansas race relations.

In Arkansas the first of these Jim Crow laws was a measure introduced in the state legislature in 1891 requiring separate passenger coaches for blacks and whites on railway trains and racially separate waiting rooms in railway passenger stations. John E. Bush was instrumental in mobilizing blacks against the separate-coach proposal. The Mosaic Templars cofounder was a key organizer of a mass protest meeting held on January 19, 1891, at Little Rock's black First Baptist Church, located at Seventh and Gaines streets in downtown Little Rock. Over six hundred persons were in attendance, and Bush chaired a special committee of race leaders that presented a number of forceful resolutions denouncing the separate-coach proposal, all of which were unanimously adopted.

In 1903 legislation was introduced in the Arkansas General Assembly to extend segregation to urban streetcar systems. Just as he had done twelve years earlier, John E. Bush helped mobilize African American opposition to the expansion of segregation in Arkansas, and once again emerged as a leader of black resistance. On March 11 a mass protest meeting was held again at Little Rock's black First Baptist Church. Bush was one of the six principal speakers at the protest meeting.

Reinforcing the protest meetings and resolutions, Arkansas blacks also tried to bring economic pressure to bear upon white leaders by organizing a series of racial boycotts against the state's urban streetcar companies. On the first day in which the streetcar law took effect, May 27, 1903, black boycotts of the state's streetcar systems were inaugurated in Little Rock, Pine Bluff, and Hot Springs. Blacks in Little Rock even organized a We Walk League, whose members agreed to submit voluntarily to fines whenever they relented and rode the streetcars. The president of the new league reportedly was a porter in a Fifth Street saloon, suggesting that the boycott effort obtained support from blacks of all social classes, even though the initial resistance to this latest onslaught of segregation had been led by middle-class spokesmen like Mosaic Templars leader John E. Bush. Black traffic on the street railways of Little Rock fell by over 90 percent, and it apparently declined precipitously in Pine Bluff and Hot Springs as well; in all three cities the boycott continued for weeks.

Despite the reverses that he and his race suffered in 1891 and 1903, Bush continued to fight against racial injustice. In 1905 a measure was introduced in the Arkansas General Assembly at the behest of then-governor Jeff Davis that would have "segregated" school-tax revenues. Under this proposal only taxes collected from blacks would be used to finance black schools. Had the segregated school-tax bill been adopted, it would virtually have destroyed public schools and public education for Arkansas's black children, particularly in Delta plantation counties where blacks constituted a large majority of the population but where land ownership and wealth were concentrated in the hands of a small minority of whites.

Among those black leaders who began to raise the alarm was John E. Bush. If there was ever a cause in which Bush fervently believed, then surely this was it. Earlier his own enrollment in Little Rock's first public school for blacks in 1869 had been the transforming event of his life. Bush, moreover, was perhaps more than any other black Arkansan suited to lead this particular fight. His own rise in the world and his leadership of the Mosaic Templars of America, an organization that controlled one of the largest concentrations of black capital in the United States—these together seemingly gave the lie to the contention of white supremacists like Jeff Davis that blacks were members of a "degenerate and improvident race" that was "not susceptible of higher education" or capable of advancement and progress.*

*Quotations are from the third inaugural address of Gov. Jeff Davis, reprinted in Marvin E. DeBoer, ed. *Dreams of Power, The Power of Dreams: The Inaugural Addresses of the Governors of Arkansas* (Fayetteville: The University of Arkansas Press, 1988.)

Bush made a public appeal against the segregated school-tax bill in a letter, "To the Senators and Representatives of the General Assembly of Arkansas," published in the Little Rock *Arkansas Gazette* on January 15, 1905. His letter was obviously directed at a white southern audience. It appealed to regional pride and emphasized the Negro's loyalty to the South and to southern whites and contributions to the southern economy. The letter also accommodated rather than challenged tradition by highlighting the role of the Negro as a laborer on the plantations. Yet in spite of its overall conservative tone, the letter also contained a threat, warning whites that adoption of the bill might lead to a mass exodus of black tenants and sharecroppers from the plantation fields. Ever since the end of the Civil War, Arkansas planters had been concerned about procuring and retaining an adequate labor force, and such a threat was probably not taken lightly. Despite strenuous efforts on its behalf by Governor Davis, the segregated school-tax proposal was overwhelmingly defeated in the Arkansas House of Representatives by a vote of fifty-six to twenty-nine: one student of the vote, historian Raymond Arsenault, has noted that most legislators were reluctant to support a measure that might exacerbate an already troublesome labor shortage.

The high regard in which John E. Bush was held also likely contributed to the final outcome. The victory, however, attested not only to Bush's stature but also to his power. The Mosaic Templars of America was a major customer of and depositor in the Little Rock banks. And Bush was a close confidant of Booker T. Washington, who had emerged as President Theodore Roosevelt's principal advisor on southern politics and on federal appointments in the southern states. One key white Democratic opponent of the segregated school-tax bill, W. W. Haynes, would owe his subsequent appointment as commander of the Arkansas National Guard to Bush's endorsement.

Governor Davis must have been bitterly disappointed over the defeat of the segregated school-tax proposal. He had invested a great deal of his personal political capital in the fight, having directly lobbied and buttonholed many of the

legislators: one irate lawmaker complained that
the governor had warned that he would ruin the
political career of anyone who opposed the measure. Just as surely, John E. Bush must have taken
great satisfaction from the defeat of the segregated school-tax bill. Remarkably, in an era of tri-
umphalist white supremacy, the black Mosaic
Templars leader had triumphed over Arkansas's
most consummate white politician.

Of all the Mosaic Templars' leaders, Bush was
by far the most politically active. On two occasions, however, the order's other cofounder,
Chester W. Keatts, entered the political fray. In
1882 Keatts ran for the office of Pulaski County
circuit clerk. Following the September 1882 election, a partisan Democratic-controlled board dis-
allowed much of the opposition vote on technical
and highly suspect grounds. Although the official
returns claimed that Keatts had lost the election
to his Democratic opponent by a vote of 3,884 to
2,567, Keatts believed, not unreasonably, that he
had been cheated out of victory. He experienced
a similar outcome when he ran in another election for judge of the police court of Little Rock.

In spite of this lack of electoral success, because
of his prominence and influence, Keatts was able
nonetheless to obtain a number of government
appointments. At various times he served as
United States deputy marshal for the Eastern
District of Arkansas, as messenger and crier in the
United States Court of Appeals, and as a deputy
constable in Big Rock Township, Pulaski County,
Arkansas. When a Little Rock streetcar company
underwent financial reorganization in 1895, Keatts
was named court-appointed receiver of the bank-
rupt firm by federal judge J. A. Williams. Keatts
posted personal bond of forty thousand dollars
and spent over a year disposing of the corporation's properties; he earned special commendation
from the bench and the general satisfaction of all
concerned.

The Mosaic Templars' traditions of political
involvement and of activism and protest did not
expire with the death of the order's founders. It
lived on especially in the person of Scipio
Africanus Jones, Little Rock's most prominent
black attorney during the early twentieth century.
Jones served as the Templars' chief legal counsel,

holding the title of National Attorney General. Like John E. Bush before him, he also was a vice-president in Booker T. Washington's National Negro Business League. Nevertheless, early in his legal career he displayed an activist streak, leading a successful suit to improve conditions for prisoners at the Pulaski County penal farm. He is best remembered today for the role he played in the aftermath of the Elaine race massacres of 1919. When violence erupted following an attempt by local black tenants and sharecroppers to organize a union near the town of Elaine in Phillips County, Arkansas, enraged whites killed dozens and perhaps hundreds of blacks; five whites also lost their lives during the violence. In the riot's wake, twelve black defendants were sentenced to death by all-white juries in trials that can only be described as travesties of justice. Displaying great personal courage, Jones, at considerable risk to himself, worked tirelessly on behalf of the twelve blacks who had been convicted and against all odds eventually secured their release.

Throughout the legal proceedings and deliberations, Jones partnered with white attorneys from Arkansas and also obtained assistance from the national office of the National Association for the Advancement of Colored People (NAACP) in New York. In addition he received support from Mosaic Templars leader John Hamilton McConico, president of the Little Rock branch of the NAACP, who "rendered invaluable aid in fighting through the courts the famous Elaine riot cases." Further help came from yet another important Mosaic Templars figure, Dr. J. G. Thornton, who served as National Medical Examiner for the Templars. During the Elaine litigation he served as chairman of a Defense Fund Commission which raised more than twelve thousand dollars to help the twelve blacks accused.

In retrospect, it seems clear that the leadership of the Mosaic Templars of America did not perceive as mutually exclusive Booker T. Washington's emphasis on black economic development and enterprise and W. E. B. Du Bois's call for continuing black political involvement and racial protest. Indeed, it was the financial security provided by the Mosaic Templars' success that enabled its leaders to champion their race's interest and battle against discrimination.

* * *

As the Mosaic Templars of America moved toward the beginning of its last full decade of existence in the United States, its future appeared bright. Chester E. Bush, the eldest son of John E. Bush, had succeeded his father and according to all accounts was serving energetically and ably as the organization's National Grand Scribe and Treasurer. The Templars continued to thrive, and when during World War I Woodrow Wilson's secretary of the treasury, William Gibbs McAdoo, attended a war bond rally in Little Rock, he was astonished when Scipio A. Jones, on the stage of the Kempner Theater, presented him with a check from the Templars order for $50,000. Jones proudly announced that if that weren't sufficient, the Mosaic Templars could raise another $50,000 in response to the nation's appeals. Eventually, the organization purchased a total of $125,000 worth of Liberty Loan bonds.

During the 1920s the Templars organization

continued to prosper and expand, and by 1924 its membership had increased to some 108,000 persons. In an article that appeared in the *Pittsburgh Courier* on June 30, 1928, it was reported as possessing approximately $800,000 in assets and as having paid out an estimated $15,000,000 in insurance claims throughout its lifetime. It had now grown to become one of the most important black-owned business enterprises in the United States and, indeed, for that era, one of the most important in the world.

Already, however, storm clouds were appearing on the horizon. Chester E. Bush died on November 18, 1924, after suffering a paralytic stroke said to have been brought on by overwork and exhaustion. His younger brother, Aldridge E. Bush, was appointed his successor and performed well. Aldridge Bush was especially admired for the history of the organization that he had recently coauthored with his fellow Mosaic Templar, P. L. Dorman. Entitled *The Mosaic Templars of America—Its Founders and Officials* and published by the Central Printing Company of Little Rock, Arkansas, the book was based on oral interviews of surviving early Templars' members and meticulous examination of official records and papers, many of which are now lost. An impressive work of scholarship, it would provide an invaluable and enduring testament to the legacy and achievements of the Mosaic Templars of America.

Nevertheless, in spite of the esteem that Aldridge Bush enjoyed, internal tensions developed when on April 13, 1925, he and his relatives brought suit in Pulaski County Chancery Court, asking the court to affirm that they owned the copyrights to the rituals of the order and asking leave to sell these copyrights to the Mosaic Templars for the sum of $150,000. They proposed to have the order pay the amount by taking $50,000 in cash from its Mortuary Fund and to issue promissory notes for the remainder of the purchase price. Altogether, the Mosaic Templars of America would be required to pay $179,000, principal and interest, for the rights claimed by the Bush family. If the order failed to make the required payments on time, then the copyrights would revert to the family.

Scipio A. Jones, the order's National Attorney General, contested these claims as an individual benefit certificate holder and won advisory opinions from the Arkansas state insurance commissioner and the Arkansas attorney general holding that transferring funds from the Mortuary Fund for this purpose would be illegal. At its National Grand Lodge meeting held in July 1925 in what would prove to be a fateful decision, the Mosaic Templars society voted to purchase the copyrights from the Bush family for $150,000, and promissory notes were executed for the purpose of underwriting the transaction with the stipulation that "the payment of said purchase price shall be made from the revenues flowing from said copyrights and contract for royalties."* (No withdrawals from the Mortuary Fund were authorized.)

While the Bush family largely carried the day in these internal wranglings, they may have

*"Complaint in Equity" and "Answer" (see Defendant's Exhibit A) *Ursaline Bush, et al. vs. Mosaic Templars of America,* in Pulaski County, Arkansas, Circuit Clerk's Office, Case No. 42659.

contributed to Aldridge E. Bush's decision to begin his own life insurance enterprise in Little Rock, the Central Life Insurance Company. The strain of attempting to direct both his new business and continue to serve as National Grand Scribe and Treasurer of the Mosaic Templars eventually proved to be too much. On September 27, 1928, Bush voluntarily resigned his post in the organization that his father had cofounded. Although his departure was amicable, it eliminated a potential conflict of interest.

The Templars might well have survived these internal troubles had it not been for the sudden onslaught of the Great Depression, beginning with the famous stock market crash on Wall Street on October 29, 1929. National unemployment soon soared to 25 percent of the work force, and among blacks, who suffered from the tradition that they would be among "the last hired and first fired," the unemployment rate was astronomical; in some cities the number of blacks who had lost their jobs and were on relief reached as high as 80 percent. The impact on black-owned insurance organizations was devastating. Younger African Americans began terminating their policies or reducing their coverage, and the older members of course continued dying. Reduced membership and a higher mortality rate proved to be an insurmountable problem. The grim statistics speak volumes: in 1918 thirty-three African American fraternal insurance providers were based in Arkansas, but by 1931 the number had plummeted to ten, and by 1937 only two remained.

The Mosaic Templars of America's own demise came in 1930 and 1931, as has been shown in a recent study by scholar Blake Wintory. Just how dire circumstances had become for the organization was revealed when its National Grand Temple, meeting in Little Rock on July 15–18, 1930, adopted an ominous resolution. The resolution specified, "any state unit or branch of the . . . corporation, which is now self-supporting and financially solvent may incorporate in such state, and . . . the title and custody of all assets . . . shall be held in trust . . . and shall speedily be disposed of and sold, and . . . the proceed shall be distributed, first for the payment of insurance claims and the residue to the state units so incorporated according to their numerical strength."*

On the very day on which the National Grand Temple concluded its deliberations, Ursaline Bush filed suit in the Pulaski County, Arkansas, Chancery Court. The widow of Chester E. Bush and the guardian for Clothilde Bush, John E. Bush, and Majorie Bush, she presented several promissory notes dated November 30, 1925, and claimed that more than twenty-four thousand dollars in principal and interest was still owed under them. In consequence of this action, the Mosaic Templars of America was placed in receivership, a form of bankruptcy.

A desperate final attempt was made to salvage what was left of the organization. According to the 1930 annual report of the State of Arkansas Insurance Department, a new group, the Modern Mosaic Templars, commenced doing business on

*Included in unpublished manuscript, Blake Wintory, "Mosaic Templars of America Exhibit Narratives," Mosaic Templars Cultural Center, Department of Arkansas Heritage, Little Rock Arkansas.

October 25, 1930, and *Polk's Little Rock and North Little Rock City Directory* for the year 1931 lists it as operating out of the original Mosaic Templars national headquarters building at West Ninth and Broadway streets. Yet, this reincarnation could no more escape the ravages of the national economic catastrophe than had its predecessor, and it quickly ceased to be mentioned in any subsequent state insurance reports or city directories.

* * *

The Mosaic Templars organization, like so many businesses, had been destroyed by the Great Depression. Its former National Temple or headquarters building in Little Rock, nevertheless, still survived. By the mid-1980s, however, it became obvious that the building's future was imperiled. Having passed through a succession of owners, the building gradually fell into disrepair, and only one commercial tenant remained on its premises. Its adjoining 1918 annex building had already perished in a fire that had occurred on October 16, 1984, and the surrounding West Ninth Street historic black business district had fallen into decay: competition from newly integrated downtown businesses, misguided policies of urban renewal, and construction of a new Federal Interstate highway that destroyed part of West Ninth Street had all hastened the neighborhood's demise.

In 1988 John Cain, a manager of Little Rock radio station KABF and the host of one of the station's jazz programs, launched a movement to save the building. In conjunction with Little Rock restaurateur Mark Abernathy, a special jazz concert featuring famed musician Wynton Marsalis was held the following year. Several thousand dollars was raised for a new Mosaic Templars building restoration fund.

Eventually, the money raised from the concert would be used to pay Little Rock historic preservation architect Tommy Jameson for the first architectural design work done to prepare for the building's restoration. Further progress occurred soon afterward when, thanks to the City of Little Rock's then Historic Preservation Administrator, Molly Satterfield, the Mosaic Templars headquarters building was listed on the National Register of Historic Places.

Just when things appeared to be advancing so

well, a crisis arose. In 1992 a local developer obtained an option to buy the building and sell it. The building would be razed, and its site used as the location for a fast-food franchise.

In May and June of that year, several hundred persons, both black and white—including African American community spokespersons, historians, historic preservationists, and other concerned citizens—attended a series of emergency meetings held on the campus of Philander Smith College. Out of these meetings a new organization was born, which on January 19, 1993, was officially chartered as a new nonprofit corporation, the Society for the Preservation of the Mosaic Templars of America Building, to be known informally as the Mosaic Templars Building Preservation Society. A new board of directors was selected, and Maud Woods, a Little Rock school administrator and teacher, became the group's first president.

The society's first challenge was simply to save the building. The group began an intensive lobbying campaign, issuing press releases, contacting state legislators, meeting with city officials, and

rallying support from various community organizations. With enthusiastic backing from the Little
Rock board of directors, these efforts led the city
to purchase the building for $110,000 in late 1993.
This marked the first time in Little Rock's history
that the city purchased a building solely for purposes of historic preservation.

Buoyed by this initial success, the preservation
society next launched an effort to have an appropriation of $185,000 included in a city-sponsored
Future Little Rock initiative for the purpose of
acquiring the lots immediately surrounding the
building. Little Rock voters passed the initiative
on December 14, 1993, assuring that the property
could be acquired and the building buffered and
protected. The society also succeeded in securing
a forty-thousand-dollar appropriation from the
city to replace the building's roof.

Next, the Mosaic Templars Building Preservation Society began initial planning for the creation of a museum of Arkansas African American
history and culture to be located in the Mosaic
Templars building, something that had always
been one of its primary objectives. Although a

preliminary agreement with a church-related community-development corporation did not progress as first hoped, the society persisted in its efforts. Subsequently, it lobbied successfully to have a projected appropriation of $3,000,000 included in the spring 1999 Building a Better Little Rock initiative. When the initiative did not prevail, the society's officers and members still refused to lose heart.

Continuing their efforts and led by their new president, Mrs. Ellen Carpenter, a retired Little Rock teacher and prominent black community leader, they achieved two important victories in 2001. With the crucial endorsement and support of the Arkansas Legislative Black Caucus and its chairman, Senator Tracy Steele, the preservation society helped win enactment of two major statutes pertaining to the Mosaic Templars building, both sponsored by state representative John Lewellen and state senator Bill Walker.

These laws appropriated monies to finance the first phase of the building's restoration and created the new Mosaic Templars Cultural Center of the Department of Arkansas Heritage, to be housed in the restored building. During the subsequent 2003 legislative session, additional appropriations were obtained for the building's restoration and to employ a new director and staff for the cultural center.

Soon after the Mosaic Templars Cultural Center began its operations, representatives of the preservation society met with Ms. Constance Sarto, the center's new director; other officers of the Department of Arkansas Heritage; and Mr. Lawrence J. Malley, the director of the University of Arkansas Press. The society proposed that, as one of its first initiatives, the Mosaic Templars Cultural Center, in collaboration with the press, sponsor republication of the original 1924 edition of A. E. Bush and P. L. Dorman's *History of the Mosaic Templars of America—Its Founders and Officials,* which had long been out of print. All parties involved embraced the preservation society's proposal with enthusiasm. Subsequently, a contract was signed under which the Heritage Department provided ten thousand dollars in subvention monies to help facilitate the project, and the preservation society itself obtained a four-thousand-dollar grant from the State of

Arkansas's Black History Advisory Committee (since renamed the Black History Commission) to help underwrite the effort.

Another welcome development occurred on February 17, 2003, when the Little Rock board of directors unanimously adopted a resolution authorizing the transfer of the Mosaic Templars building's ownership to the State of Arkansas and the Department of Arkansas Heritage. Shortly thereafter, Mayor Jim Dailey signed the transfer deed, and at long last actual restoration work on the building began.

Then, tragically just as the initial phase of the building's restoration had started, transients entered the building and ignited a fire early in the morning of March 16, 2005, and within minutes the historic structure was almost totally destroyed.

Devastated, the board of the Mosaic Templars Building Preservation Society met the following evening. Even in this time of greatest distress, its members refused to surrender hope. It adopted a resolution urging the state to reconstruct the building, and before the week was out a press conference was held in the rotunda of the Arkansas State Capitol. Participants at the press conference included the preservation society's president, Mrs. Ellen Carpenter, and other officers and directors of the society; Little Rock's mayor, Jim Dailey; Cathie Remmel Matthews, director of the Department of Arkansas Heritage; and members of the Arkansas Legislative Black Caucus. All pledged their backing for reconstruction of the building and renewed their support for the Mosaic Templars Cultural Center.

Financed with further legislative monies and substantial grants from the Arkansas Natural and Cultural Resources Council of the State of Arkansas, construction of the building soon commenced and is now complete. Located on the same site as that of the previous 1913 Mosaic Templars headquarters building and its 1918 annex, the new structure's exterior facades very nearly replicate those of the original two buildings. Its second-floor offices and third-floor auditorium, moreover, closely resemble and are a faithful facsimile of those features of the 1913 edifice. A grand opening ceremony is now planned for September 19 and 20, 2008.

* * *

Postscript

When the Mosaic Templars of America went into receivership and ceased functioning as a national organization in the United States in 1930 and 1931, an organization that had once been a true exemplar of black achievement had disappeared into the mists of the past—or so it was long thought. Soon after establishing its own internet website, however, the Mosaic Templars Building Preservation Society received on November 16, 1999, an inquiry from Loyal Woods Temple Number 25 of the Grand United Order of Mosaic Templars in Barbados, West Indies. Possibly the last surviving chapter of the Mosaic Templars organization in the world, it asked for any information pertaining to the Mosaic Templars early origins and history. Stunned—and ecstatic—the members of the preservation society began an extensive correspondence with the Barbados group. On the occasion of the Loyal Woods Temple's seventy-fifth anniversary celebration, six members of the preservation society—John Cain, Andre Louis Guerrero, Mary Lois Hardin, Linda

Kamara, Constance Sarto, and this writer—flew to the island to participate in the festivities. They attended a special black-tie anniversary banquet and awards ceremony held at the Emerald Palm Restaurant at Porters, St. James, Barbados, on Saturday, October 25, 2003, presenting to Brother Hilary Bruce, the Grand Mosaic Master of Barbados, and Brother Richard Crichlow, Worthy Mosaic Master of the Loyal Woods Temple , three newly struck bronze medallions from the City of Little Rock. They also read aloud congratulatory letters from Mike Huckabee, governor of Arkansas, and Cathie Remmel Matthews, director of the Department of Arkansas Heritage. In turn, the members of the Loyal Woods chapter presented to the Mosaic Templars Building Preservation Society a handsome plaque carved from rare Barbadian mahogany. Two members of the preservation society, Andre Louis Guerrero and this author, were able to remain in Barbados for several days after the banquet and be initiated into the Loyal Woods lodge. They were likely the first persons from the place of its origin to become members of the Mosaic Templars order in some seventy-two years. Since the anniversary celebration, members of the preservation society and the Loyal Woods chapter have remained in close communication. Plans are being made to have a delegation from Barbados attend the grand opening of the reconstructed Mosaic Templars headquarters building and the Mosaic Templars Cultural Center in 2008. The presence of these cherished persons, perhaps among the last living Mosaic Templars on earth, will be a singular and moving feature of the dedication ceremony.

History of the Mosaic Templars of America

Its Founders and Officials

A. E. BUSH   P. L. DORMAN

History of the Mosaic Templars of America—Its Founders and Officials

EDITED BY

A. E. BUSH AND P. L. DORMAN

LITTLE ROCK
CENTRAL PRINTING COMPANY
1924

Printed in United States of America

CONTENTS

ILLUSTRATIONS

FOREWORD

After the first celebration of Founder's Day, May 22, 1923, constant and urgent requests came from many of our friends and from those who were anxious to know, asking that we compile a history of the Organization, that might be accepted as authentic, covering its record from its incipiency up to the present date. Yielding to these requests, we have endeavored to record the principal events, both in the lives of the FOUNDERS and in the development of the Order. We feel that this is sufficient justification for relating the story.

For the labor and care that have been taken in the preparation of this book, we shall feel remunerated if it only gives to the readers, and to the race, greater faith and hope in racial endeavors; if it will serve as a call to the discouraged and weak, urging them to continue their onward march and work out their own destinies by persistent effort.

There is a tendency, from many outside sources, to desregard and belittle Negro history and to deny in full, all outstanding achievements of the race. The Negro race has been a liberal contributor to the civilization of the world, but by shrewd manipulations of the writers of modern history he has been robbed of much of this honor.

The writers will therefore feel bountifully repaid if this book shall only play a slight part in helping those who are broken in spirit to be of good cheer and hope, and to dedicate themselves to the service of their race.

We make no special claim for any literary merit in the production of this work, but have been content to merely give in sequence, a true and simple narrative of the work of the Order, not only for the enlightenment of the present membership, but for generations unborn.

Chapter I

LIFE SKETCH OF THE HONORABLES CHESTER W. KEATTS AND JOHN EDWARD BUSH

In this humble effort to give a simple, but accurate account of the history of the Mosaic Templars of America, it will be impossible to divorce the names and the life history of the two men who had more to do with the creation and the successful accomplishments of the Order than any other persons—the Honorables J. E. Bush and C. W. Keatts, whose names will be forever inseparably connected with the Mosaic Templars of America; men who by their vision and by their confidence in the race to follow proper leadership, have made this particular Order take front rank in all fraternal efforts of the Negro race.

At the time when these men attempted to organize the Mosaic Templars of America, fraternal organizations among colored people were in most cases failures, especially was this true in Arkansas. The Masons and Odd

Fellows were probably the most outstanding examples of fraternal effort among our people in this State. There were many nondescript bodies, calling themselves fraternities, but in most cases had no program for perpetuity. They merely existed or were promoted for the sole benefit of the promoters. It was a common practice that after organization and the accumulation of funds, to loot the treasury and then disband. At that time State laws were inadequate to give proper protection for safeguarding the interest of the members.

Mr. Bush in early manhood had made a reputation among his people as a man of rugged honesty and indomitable courage. He had little patience with inefficiency and dishonesty. With firm conviction that something should be done to save the race from those who were exploiting it day by day, and that order should be brought out of the then chaotic fraternal conditions, he set about to put into execution these convictions, and here fate came to his aid and suggested the remedy, which will be told in subsequent chapters.

C. W. KEATTS (Deceased)

FOUNDER

HONORABLE CHESTER W. KEATTS

The late Chester W. Keatts, the co-founder, and regarded by all as the co-equal of Hon. J. E. Bush, was born near Little Rock, Pulaski County, Arkansas, in the year 1854, of slave parents. The exact date of his birth is not known, because in those days not much, if any, record was kept of births. Because of his parents being in humble circumstances he was forced to make his own provisions for an education and also to assist in taking care of his mother. Chester was the only boy child, so you can readily appreciate the heavy burden that must have been naturally placed upon him in caring for himself and mother. By hard work, diligent study and a determination to do, he succeeded in completing his common school education in 1874. His education was not handed him on a silver platter, but his efforts developed in him his mental, as well as moral powers. He was naturally of a bright mind and had only to be given the slightest chance and he would render a good account of himself. Mr. Keatts not only had a good common school learning, but was educated in the ways of the world; and as one supplements the other, a well balanced man must necessarily have the advantages that both give; so had Mr. Keatts.

His main means of support in his early days was gotten through farming, at which vocation he remained until he reached the age of twenty-four years. As the art of farming was so deeply instilled in him from childhood, Mr. Keatts in subsequent years found it quite difficult to refrain absolutely from it and as a result of this attachment he purchased a beautiful stretch of land just northwest of the city and up to his death kept it in an excellent state of cultivation.

In the year of 1875 he entered the U. S. railway mail service as a clerk. In this service he had the honor of being promoted three times. This position was held by him, with honor, for seventeen years. During his employ as railway clerk, with his co-partner, Mr. Bush, the idea of founding the Mosaic Templars of America was conceived and materialized. Like that of his friend, J. E. Bush, the appointment to the mail service was his first Government position of trust.

During the early 90's he ran for the office of circuit clerk of Pulaski County, Arkansas, and was elected by an overwhelming majority vote, but was counted out by the opposing party after a very heated contest. His next political accomplishment came by having the honor of being appointed and serving as messenger and crier in the United States Court of Appeals under Judge H. C. Caldwell. This appointment came directly through Judge Caldwell.

The most outstanding appointment for this illustrious person, and an appointment without parallel as far as the race was concerned, was when he was appointed receiver of the Little Rock Traction and Electric Company in 1895 by Hon. J. A. Williams, Judge of the United States District Court. He was required to make a bond of $40,000.00 which he made by virtue of his personal holdings and prominent and honorable standing in his community. This receivership required his attention for more than a year and placed upon him a severe test of ability. However, he entered upon these duties with that same masterly determination that characterized his life and he was discharged from the receivership with due credit, after properly disposing of the properties of the company and making a satisfactory report to the Court.

Mr. Keatts also served as a deputy constable of Big Rock Township, Arkansas, for a number of years. He served most creditably in this capacity. Among his other political achievements was the race for judge of the police court of Little Rock. His poll of votes in this particular race was the same as that of circuit clerk, he was elected by a very large majority but was counted out. On November 4, 1876, he was appointed U. S. deputy marshal for the Eastern District of Arkansas.

The political career of Mr. Keatts shows him very brilliant and is marked by his fidelity to the principles and interests of the Republican party. In his community, he was respected by both white and colored for his sterling qualities, capability, energy and faithfulness to duty, irrespective to his service in either a public or private capacity. In his long employ in the postal service, he ranked second to none in efficiency; and in his political career he was recognized as a leader in his State.

Mr. Keatts was a staunch member of the First Baptist Church of Little Rock and served as one of its trustees until his death. He believed in a practical, as well as a revealed religion. He was also affiliated with such secret societies as the Masons, Odd Fellows and Knights of Pythias.

On December 3, 1881, Mr. Keatts was married to Miss Mary Warren in the city of Little Rock, Ark. She is a woman possessed of education and ability, and served in the city schools of Little Rock for a number of years. Through her devotion, cheerful assistance and co-operation, Mr. Keatts was successful in accumulating a comfortable fortune. He was conservatively estimated as being worth $50,000.00 in real and personal property at the time of his death.

From the birth of the Mosaic Templars of America until his death, he was its National Grand Master and under his leadership the organization grew from thirteen members to over 25,000 members. His administration in office covered a period of twenty-six years, all of which time he retained the confidence and respect of his many followers.

As a result of his persistent labors he suffered with a complete breakdown in health and his death followed January 16, 1908, at his family residence in the city of Little Rock, Arkansas, which marked the close of a useful life. He was buried with full Mosaic honors in the Fraternal Cemetery on January 20, 1908, being survived by his wife and aged mother.

J. E. BUSH (Deceased)
FOUNDER

HONORABLE JOHN E. BUSH

The late John E. Bush was born in the little town of Moscow, Tennessee, which is today not much larger than it was at the time of his birth, which was November 15, 1856. Like many other slave children, he knew little of his father. With his mother, sisters and brothers he was brought to Arkansas by his owners, who fled Tennessee at the approach of the Federal troops. During the Civil War it was the usual practice of slave owners to move at the approach of the Yankees, as the Federal troops were called, all of their personal property, which included their slaves, to more secure territory. The South at that time still held to the hope of the ultimate triumph of their armies and the perpetuation of slavery. These people were known as "Refugees." This happened in the year 1862. Little Johnnie, as he was then called, suffered all of the hardships incident to such a flight. In those days there was no direct rail communication into Arkansas from Moscow, Tennessee.

When freedom came the only legacy that came to young Bush and his mother was hard work and all of the hardships incident to the period following the close of the Civil War, for Arkansas, like most of the other Southern States, had been practically bankrupted through the four-years period of strife. The hardships undergone by the family developed in young Bush moral courage, self-reliance and a strong determination to break down every barrier which confronted him.

His education, by reason of the limited opportunities then offered in the State for Negroes, and the poverty of the family, was very limited as far as the schoolroom went, but in the university of hard knocks and experience, he put in full time and came out well prepared for the role that he would assume in later years. The only academic training he received was in the public schools of Little Rock, which at that time had a very limited curriculum. While in the public school he showed the same courage and self-reliance that had been noticed in him as a little slave boy.

Under the strain, incident to the times and hard existing conditions, his mother succumbed under the unequal struggle and left him an orphan at the age of seven years and from that time as he so often put it in his later years it was with him a case of "Root, hog, or die."

When he had grown older, the desire to get out of school all that was offered was uppermost in his mind and he became a brickyard worker, and soon had mastered the art of brick moulder. With the money earned in this way during the summer months he found it possible to continue in school and in the year 1876 he was one of the honor graduates.

Immediately upon graduation he was appointed principal of the Capitol Hill public school, which in those days was no small honor. This school stands today on the same site which it occupied in '76. In 1878 he accepted the principalship of the colored public school in Hot Springs, serving through the year 1879.

While his career was short, by reason of his conscientious attitude in this work he attracted the attention of the more thoughtful of both races who realized that there had come on the scene a dependable and competent young man who bore all the earmarks of a young man who would be heard from in the future. His termination of an active career in the schoolroom did not diminish his interest in the educational interest of his people and up to the time of his death he was the special champion of the cause of the colored teachers and colored children of his home city.

On June 18, 1879, Mr. Bush was married to Miss Cora Winfrey, daughter of Solomon and Rebecca Winfrey, one of Little Rock's old and most highly respected families, and much of the success he attained in latter life can be attributed to the untiring, unselfish devotion and unbounded faith that she had in her young husband. To their union was born seven children, three of whom survive— Mrs. Stella Bush-Brown, Chester E., and Aldridge E. Bush.

Mr. Bush, though fortunate in saving sufficient wealth to provide reasonably well for
his family, was thoroughly practicable and
practiced by example what he so often
preached to others, that the young people of
the race should be taught the dignity of labor,
and from the time that his children were old
enough he had them by his side taking part
in his varied business enterprises, and demanded of them the same exacting service
that he did from all others who were in his
employ. Each of his children has always
been active in some capacity in the Order
which he founded and loved so well. At his
passing away the mantle of his leadership in
the Order fell on the shoulders of his sons and
they have made worthy successors of their
father's efforts.

MR. BUSH IN POLITICS

Every man has his "hobby". The "hobby"
of Mr. Bush was politics. He took as naturally to the political game as the proverbial
duck would take to water. Even in years

after, when fortune had smiled upon him, he was still active and fought harder than ever, first for the interest of his race and secondly because he loved fighting in this particular field, and throughout his long and honorable career few were the defeats that could be chalked against his record. Trained in a school of relentless political warfare, Mr. Bush was intensely partisan and uncompromising. He never forgot a friend and seldom forgave politically, an enemy, not personal, but to the party cause. It is difficult for a man to be active as long as he had been, in party politics, without creating enemies, but up to the time of his retirement from the field by reason of ill health he still maintained his hold on the party. He was one of the few prominent colored men of the South to survive the advent of the lily white movement. He was the last colored man to go to a National Republican Convention as one of the "Big Four" from this State. He fought to the bitter end the foes of the colored men within the party, but was never a bolter. He established a reputation for political honesty, with friend and foe, and his political garments were never besmirched with the charge of graft or double-crossing when he had once given his word or promise. He was scarcely more than twenty-one years old when he entered the political arena and from that time on through a period covering more than thirty years he was on the firing line in the defense of his race and the party of his choice.

His first political appointment came when he was given the position of railway postal clerk, in the United States railway mail service. At that time these appointments were not made through the civil service regulations but were the results of the political pull which one might have, or through their friends' influence with the political powers that be. In this service as in former occupations he had an untarnished record. His record for efficiency was such that he was recommended for clerk-in-charge, and was promptly indorsed for the same through the Republican State Central Committee. Such indorsement then was equivalent to appointment. He received the promotion and remained as such for seventeen years, after which time, he, of his own volition, asked to be retired.

APPOINTED RECEIVER OF UNITED STATES LAND OFFICE AT LITTLE ROCK BY PRESIDENT MCKINLEY

In 1898 Mr. Bush's first major appointment came with his appointment as receiver of the land office at Little Rock under the administration of President McKinley. Though the movement against the appointment of Negroes to Federal position had gained impetus throughout the South, not only by Democrats but by a large element of white Republicans, Mr. Bush's appointment to this position was received with much delight by both elements. Though one of the best known men in his State, this appointment in the face of the general opposition to the appointment of colored men to office in the South attracted national attention and Mr. Bush became at once a national figure among the members of his race.

The one dominant passion with Mr. Bush was to seize every point of vantage to do something for his race and in his position as receiver of the land office he found splendid opportunities. There were many thousands of acres of fertile lands in the State owned by the Government and open to "homesteading." Aside from the official routine of advertising these lands, Mr. Bush personally went about to public meetings and colored churches advising them to take advantage of the opportunity of "homesteading" this valuable land. The result of his efforts is that some of the best farms in Arkansas are today owned by colored people.

FIGHTS HIS GREATEST POLITCAL BATTLE

The first administration of the land office passed without incident. Under the administration of President Roosevelt, Mr. Bush was a candidate to succeed himself. His splendid administration of the affairs of the office made him his logical successor. Those who had their hand on the party pulse conceded this without debate. He had received the party indorsement, but schism had broken out within the party. The lily white movement had been born and had reached large proportions within the party, and there was competition from this element. They put forward a candidate of their own. The fight was on, and precipitated one of the most bitter contests in the annals of State party politics.

Affairs took an unlooked-for turn and Mr. Bush found that he had powerful opposition from some of the members of his own race, and strangely from without the State by a group of men styled the "Intellectuals" of the race. Their headquarters were in Boston. Mr. Bush was marked for slaughter by this group by reason of his close friendship with the late Dr. Booker T. Washington. By reason of Mr. Bush's prestige and the fact that it was generally accepted that Dr. Washington was unofficially the referee of President Roosevelt in political appointments, and the uncompromising attitude of this group to the ascendency of Dr. Washington, Mr. Bush found that he was a victim of the hatred of this particular group. For many weeks an acrimonious warfare was kept up against him in this group's particular organ published in Boston. Wild and unfounded charges were published against him. In this they were aided and abetted by a small group of disappointed and disgruntled colored men in his own home city, and several within the State. This fight attracted national attention. Mr. Bush did not quail before this onslaught of the opposition but cleared the decks for one of the most memorable fights in State party politics.

When it became generally known that Mr. Bush had opposition, he was deluged with letters, telegrams and proffers of aid from men of both races and both parties. The white people of Little Rock, especially of the opposite party, volunteered their testimony to the fitness of Mr. Bush for this important position and indorsed his reappointment.

Notable among these indorsements is the following from the then mayor, and from the city clerk of Little Rock, both Democrats. Mayor Duly wrote as follows:

Little Rock, Nov. 10, 1901.

Mr. President:

HON. SIR—Mr. J. E. Bush (col.), present incumbent of the office of receiver of lands, located in this city informs me that he is an applicant for re-appointment, knowing him personally, and his standing in this community, I have no hesitancy in recommending him for the position.

Most respectfully,

W. R. DULEY, *Mayor.*

To Hon. Theo. Roosevelt,

President, U. S.

The city clerk contributed the following testimonial:

Little Rock, Nov. 4, 1901.

Honorable Theo. Roosevelt, President of the United States, Washington, D. C.

DEAR SIR—This will serve to recommend Mr. J. E. Bush, of this city, who applies for reappointment to the office of receiver of United States land, with whom I am personally acquainted and know him to be above the average and a colored man that is very prominent among all classes of both colors.

Very respectfully,

F. M. OLIVER, *City Clerk.*

To publish all the testimonials given Mr. Bush for re-appointment would require a good-sized book. Among the many Mr. Bush always highly prized the following coming from one of the large planters of the county:

Little Rock, Ark., Feb. 21, 1902.
Mr. E. A. Hitchcock, Sec. of the Interior, Washington, D. C.

MY DEAR SIR—From newspaper reports and reports that I have heard here I fear that an unintentional injustice may be done a very worthy man. While I usually take no hand whatever in matters of this kind, I have felt it my duty to write you. John E. Bush the present receiver of the U. S. land office at Little Rock, I have known for twenty-five years. For a great many years he lived a neighbor to me; I know his personal habits, his family relations, and his general conduct and reputation as a citizen. He is a colored man who stands as a leader of his race in this State. From a boy he has shown thrift and enterprise; has accumulated property, nicely educated his family and is one of those colored men who has always counseled his people to live on friendly terms with their white neighbors.

In the distribution of the federal patronage of this State when the Republican party is in power this office has always been filled by a colored man and it is to their credit that it has always been filled by a man who has not only made a good officer but has been acceptable to the white people. I understand that some old charges have been raked up against Mr. Bush. I can say to you that there is absolutely nothing in them and never was. It is reported here that his principal opponents are W. D. Matthews and Patrick Raleigh. If this office was left to be filled by election and by taxpayers of this community or of this land district were to vote, I firmly believe that Mr. Bush would receive more votes than both his opponents. I have absolutely no personal interest in this matter whatever; I affiliate with the Democratic party myself, but I do feel enough interest in the Government that I would regret to see a good man turned down and one less worthy succeed him, especially after the methods that have been adopted to besmirch his character.

Very truly yours,

JNO. R. FRAZIER, Planter.

The unwarranted attack on Mr. Bush's reappointment by the group already mentioned aroused the citizens of Little Rock, both white and colored.

The bar of Little Rock, every bank in the city, business houses without exception and the Little Rock Board of Trade gave their unqualified indorsement to his reappointment, notwithstanding his principal opponents were white men.

Probably no man in the Republican party in the State gave the Democrats more trouble than Mr. Bush, yet the Democratic Central Committee gave their strongest indorsement to him. The chairman and the secretary of this committee writing individual indorsements.

Little Rock, Nov. 7, 1901.

To the Hon. Theodore Roosevelt, President of the United States.

DEAR SIR—It affords me pleasure to indorse the application of John E. Bush for reappointment as receiver of the U. S. land office. I have known him for twenty-five years (we were boys together) as one of the leading colored citizens of this city and he has the confidence of both white and colored people here. He is to my personal knowledge a credit to his race and to the community. I think his reappointment will give general satisfaction.

I would prefer to have a Democrat but as we can't, I will let it go at that.

Very respectfully,

HORACE G. DALE,

Chm. Dem. County Central Com.

Little Rock, Nov. 11, 1901.

Hon Theodore Roosevelt, President of the United States, Washington, D. C.

DEAR SIR—It is with pleasure that I add my indorsement to the candidacy of the Hon. J. E. Bush,

of this city, as receiver of the United States Land
Office at Little Rock. I have known Mr. Bush for
thirty years, and during that time I have never heard
one word against his character. To the contrary, I
know him to be a law-abiding citizen. He is a
colored man of whom we are all justly proud; he
stands well in this community, and is a credit to his
race. He is one of the foremost colored men in the
State, and his appointment would be satisfactory to
the public generally, without regard to politics. I
indorse every word said by Mr. Dale, chairman of the
Democratic Central Committee of Pulaski County.

Very truly,

F. J. GINOCCHIO,
Secretary of Dem. Central Committee,
Pulaski County, Arkansas.

The testimonials given here are typical of
hundreds received and show the great interest
aroused concerning his reappointment and the
high esteem in which he was held by those
who knew him best.

Mr. Bush throughout his long and honorable political career had the hearty support of
General Powell Clayton who up to the time
of his death was not only one of the outstanding citizens of the State of Arkansas, but was
the dominant figure in the Republican party

in the State. At this time General Clayton was Ambassador to Mexico, but found time to go to Washington and personally see President Roosevelt in the interest of Mr. Bush. General Clayton was very indignant that outside forces should meddle into the affairs of the State and had no sympathy with the applicants of his own race for this particular position. Those who knew General Clayton knew that he was uncompromising when once he had reached a decision and the outcome was never in doubt.

Mr. Bush took much pride in the fact that the real race leaders of national prominence were his loyal friends. Such men as the late Judge M. W. Gibbs and Dr. Booker T. Washington, Allison Sweeney of the Freeman, the editor of the New York Age and many others whose names shine out on the pages of racial endeavor, were his staunch supporters.

It is an ill wind that blows nobody good and the unreasonable fight precipitated upon Mr. Bush only served to reveal the sturdy character of the man; when the battle was over he stood, revealed in the light of the most searching investigation, with a character untarnished by those who would besmirch him.

One of the most active applicants for Mr. Bush's place was W. D. Mathews, a white Republican who had brought into play every resource to secure the appointment. The following special dispatch to the St. Louis Globe-Democrat shows how the white Democrats repudiated their indorsement of Mr. Mathews.

ARKANSAS PATRONAGE FIGHT

ARKANSAS REPUBLICANS MAKING A STIR IN
WASHINGTON

W. D. Mathews Accused of Obtaining Indorsement
for Business Purposes and Using Them in
a Political Way.

Special to the Globe-Democrat.

Washington, January 22.—Mr. H. L. Remmel, chairman of the Republican State Central Committee of Arkansas, has arrived in Washington. His appearance has furnished new vigor to the contest that has been going on over Arkansas appointments to federal positions. Recently W. D. Matthews, C. P. Auten and B. M. Foreman arrived here and began a fight against the reappointment of the present federal office-holders in Arkansas and general opposition to

the Republican State committee.   Since Chairman
Remmel's arrival the contest has become exciting,
and some interesting charges have been placed in cir-
culation.   Mr. Matthews is an applicant for the appointment as receiver of the land office at Little Rock
to succeed J. E. Bush.   Additional interest was lent
to the contest today by the publication in Washington papers of a telegram announcing that Mr.
Bush had been assassinated.   Later in the day telegrams came from Mr. Bush indicating that he was
very much alive.

It is charged that Mr. Matthews, before coming to
Washington circulated the report in Little Rock that
he was going to leave the State to engage in the insurance business in Oklahoma.   It is said that in order
to secure references for his new position he secured
letters of indorsement from many Little Rock citizens
recommending him to the consideration of any with
whom he might have business.   Many of these letters
have appeared in the interior department in Washington in connection with Mr. Matthews' appointment.
The discovery of this use of the letters caused considerable correspondence, and telegrams have been received at the interior department withdrawing indorsement given to Mr. Matthews, when he was,
according to the reports, soliciting indorsements for
purely political instead of business purposes.   Among
those who have sent letters or telegrams withdrawing
their recommendation of Mr. Matthews are ex-Gov.
Dan W. Jones, Maj.-Gen. W. H. Haines, of the
Arkansas National Guard; W. C. Tipton, State
Treasurer; J. R. Jobe, State Printer; J. H. Page,
Secretary State Board of Charities; O. C. Ludwig,

Assistant Secretary of State; A. C. Hull, former Secretary of State; former Governor James P. Clarke, who is candidate for U. S. Senate; William M. Kavanaugh, County Judge of Pulaski County; Judge U. M. Rose, president of the American Bar Association, and James Mitchell, a Little Rock editor.   It is understood that a majority of the letter writers were Democrats.   Further interesting developments in the case are promised.

All of the officials named in this special dispatch to the Globe-Democrat were Democratic office-holders and merely add emphasis to the standing of Mr. Bush in his home city.

The Arkansas Democrat, daily paper published in Little Rock, made the following comment on the reported assassination of Mr. Bush:

HE IS VERY MUCH ALIVE

But John E. Bush Can See How His Death Would Have Been Regretted.

Explanation has already been made of how a bulletin was sent out Tuesday night erroneously announcing that John E. Bush, receiver of the United States land office in this city, had been assassinated. Notwithstanding that a second bulletin followed within twenty minutes announcing that it was a nephew of Receiver Bush that was killed, some of the earlier editions of the paper used the first item. In consequence of this Receiver Bush's friends have received numerous telegrams expressing regret at the supposed occurrence thus heralded. One of these telegrams came to Editor D. G. Hill, of the American Guide, from President W. B. Ferguson of the Lincoln Club. It reads:

Fort Wayne, Indiana, January 23.

D. G. Hill, Editor of the American Guide, Little Rock, Arkansas.

Have just learned of Bush's death. I wish to extend my sympathy to his family and the colored people of Arkansas in the loss of a leader of high character and sound judgment.

Signed)   W. B. FERGUSON.

This is only one of a number of telegrams along the same line. Mr. Ferguson had evidently seen the first bulletin, and not the second one.

Those parties in Washington who wanted the successor of John E. Bush appointed because of the latter's assassination resorted to a very mean trick to get an office.

In the midst of the fight the following telegram was received:

Washington, D. C., April 23, 1902.

Hon. J. E. Bush, Little Rock, Arkansas.

You and other land officers recommended by the committee appointed today. Hearty congratulations.

(Signed)   POWELL CLAYTON.

Thus ended one of the most spectacular fights in the annals of the party in the State of Arkansas. The searchlight of public scrutiny by merciless political enemies had been turned on every phase of Mr. Bush's public and private life and he stood out in bold relief without a blemish; his enemies had been discredited on every point. The following comment was made just after this appointment by one of the leading Democratic dailies of Little Rock:

J. E. BUSH, RECEIVER U. S. LAND OFFICE

The office of receiver of the United States land office is one of great importance in many ways, and it is essential to the best interest of the people generally that there should be selected men for that position who have a full realization of the duties devolving upon them—men of whose integrity there is absolutely no question and upon whom the Government may absolutely rely to use their best endeavors to prevent frauds in connection with the public lands set aside for the use of citizens upon which to build homes. As receiver of the land office in Little Rock a man has been appointed who embodies all of the requirements of an ideal official in the person of the Hon. J. E. Bush, a colored man, who was named receiver in 1898, and who has most satisfactorily filled the position during the intervening time. Mr.

W. M. EZELL
Grand Master of Oklahoma.

A native of Tennessee. Came to Little Rock in 1891 and became an active and a useful citizen. He went to Oklahoma in the pioneer days, conducted a successful retail business.

Was elected State Grand Master in 1915 at Grand Lodge meeting in Muskogee.

Number of lodges when elected, 40.

Membership, 900.

Now increased to 115 lodges with a membership of nearly 4,000.

The organization under him has bought valuable property to be used for the purpose of erecting a State Temple Building.

Bush is a man of wide experience in all public affairs and brings to the office of public receiver a thorough knowledge of conditions prevailing in the State, and the duties devolving upon him. But, notwithstanding the distinction of having been chosen for political preferment and named by President McKinley as receiver of the local land office, Mr. Bush is prouder of his achievements in behalf of his race and especially of the fact that he is one of the founders of the Mosaic Templars of America, an Order which has assumed national scope and which now has about 40,000 members in good standing. It was organized in 1882 for the purpose of elevating the colored race, socially, morally, intellectually and financially, the fraternal features have exerted a strong influence in assisting the colored people in realizing their true position and to assume the responsibilities resting upon them. This has been the life aim of Mr. Bush and it is but natural that he should be particularly gratified that through his efforts that so many of the people should have been materially assisted in many ways. His position is now that of a national character through the operation of the Mosaic Templars of America, a strictly colored people's organization, without any of the features or elements of the ritualistic work of the various secret organizations of white people, something of which the founders of the Order are proud. In fact, Mr. Bush maintains that to steal the ritual of secret orders from others is far worse than robbing a hen-roost at night—smaller and meaner. Mr. Bush is national secretary of the Mosaic Templars of America, a position he has held continuously since it is organization. Little Rock is the headquarters of the organization, C. W. Keatts being national president.   Mr. Bush is a large property owner in Little Rock and assists on every occasion in all projects looking to the upbuilding of the city, showing his loyal public spirit for the city which has so long been his home.

Mr. Bush served throughout President Roosevelt's administration and was reappointed by President Taft and continued until the defeat of the party in the national election which ushered in the Wilson administration.   Having been out of office so long Democratic aspirants immediately set up a cry for Republican resignations in order that the faithful might come into their reward.   The Mosaic Templars had grown so strong that the entire services of Mr. Bush were urgently needed in that organization, but notwithstanding this he resolutely refused to resign, having several months yet to serve of his term. As the term for which he was appointed was nearing the end he tendered his resignation to President Wilson which of course was graciously accepted, much to the gratification of those who hoped to succeed him.

In all Mr. Bush served in this office continuously for a period covering sixteen years and
through three different administrations, with
credit to himself and race. His one obsession
seemed that he was not filling this office for
himself, personally, but that in him, through
this position, the race was on trial and for
this cause alone he must not fail.

Mr. Bush had long desired to divorce himself from political activity and devote his entire time to the one thing that had become his
life's ambition, to build the Mosaic Templar
organization where it would take first place
in the rank of colored fraternities of the
world. This ambition was being rapidly realized, but he saw plainly the efforts being made
to completely silence the colored man in the
Republican party of his State with the advent
of the lily white movement and he had determined to not surrender his people to this new
challenge within the party. This was the
patent cause for the memorable fight that he
had made for reappointment.

Finding himself free by reason of the political change, he concentrated all of his efforts
in building the Order which he loved so well.
The long experience which he had as a Government employee under its most exacting regulations peculiarly fitted him for the very exacting duties devolving upon him as National
Grand Scribe of the organization. The great
period of expansion was on in the Order. The
Order under the old system had outgrown the
rules and regulations provided for the conduct of the business and he at once revolution-
ized the entire system.

He had a peculiar knack of selecting men
and seldom failed in his judgment. He surrounded himself with an intelligent array of
young men and women and set to work with
a zeal that only a man of his type could command. He was an ardent apostle of the
"strenuous life" and the Order grew by leaps
and bounds. In the office Mr. Bush was a
stern disciplinarian, yet filled with the milk of
human kindness. He was respected and
obeyed by all subordinates who loved him to

the end. His long political career made him uncompromising in all that he undertook; he trained under political masters who showed no quarter to the enemy, and yet the charge has never been brought against him that he ever forsook a friend. He brought these convictions into the office of the organization and soon built up one of the most complete working units to be found in the race.

Aside from Mr. Bush's political activity and his fraternal organization he was always active in every cause for the promotion of the interest of his people within and without the State.

A NATIONAL FIGURE

For a number of years before the Mosaic Templars had reached the fame that it was now enjoying under the direct leadership of Mr. Bush, he had enjoyed a national reputation. Always active and aggressive, never taking a neutral position on any question with which he was concerned, with a vision far in advance of the average man of affairs, he was much in demand as a speaker in national meetings of the race. It may appear paradoxical when it is recalled that his life had largely been spent in the field of politics, yet he was an ardent disciple of the doctrines of the late Dr. Booker T. Washington and for a number of years enjoyed his intimate friendship and personal confidence. He was invited by Dr. Washington to deliver the annual commencement address at one of the annual closings of this famous institution. This in itself was no small honor and attests to the standing of the man. The address was well received and received much comment throughout the press of the country. This address shows more clearly than anything that the writer could say, his position on the economic status of the race. He spoke as follows:

Mr. President, Ladies and Gentlemen:

By invitation of your most worthy president, Mr. Washington, I was invited to address you and Tuskegee graduates. I feel that I have been greatly honored by an invitation from so great a man. I have for this occasion selected as my subject, "The Negro and His Relation to the United States, Especially the Southern States." Under this head I shall speak of him as a Slave, and as a Freeman.

AS A SLAVE

If we are to believe history, the Negro's appearance on the American continent was almost simultaneous with that of the white man. The white man came here to escape persecution and oppression, both religious and political. And I hear him now as he voices that soul-inspiring sentiment through the immortal Patrick Henry, "Give me liberty or give me death." The white man knew the ills of oppression, he had seen them, felt them, and galled beneath the English yoke that bound him as a slave. He had wept that others might weep with him, and prayed that the God of Liberty would give him freedom, with all of its attributes, or give him death. And upon this proposition he stakes his life, his wife and children and bade farewell to his fatherland and departed. The beautiful scenes of vale and hill with their transcendent beauty arose before him like the phantoms of departed joys. The cherished memories of loved ones at home, and the bitter recollection of relentless warfare, were but agencies to cheer him on, nothing daunted or made him fearful. His foremost thought was liberty and freedom. Death was on every living thing, oppression in every heart, bloodshed upon every doorsill. The chilly blasts of winter blew through his curly locks, blood-stained feet marked his pathway, and at night the snow banked hill and vale made for him his couch. This in part formed the royal road to the American white man's liberty. With this liberty gained he established a republic, the greatest, grandest, and most magnificent in the world; his flag, he styled, the stars and stripes, and it sweeps the ground and touches

the stars. When once put it remains put. His
country is the home of the brave and the free. In
all of his conflicts, privations and strifes, the Negro
proved his loyalty to country, his unswerving love
and devotion to him who held him as a slave. The
profoundest mystery of the American white man
was to the outer world. How could he, with a heart
of love, with the sensibilities of a God, with a will
for liberty that knew no bounds, hold in abject
slavery the black man for two hundred and fifty
years? The white men himself could not understand it; but it was God's way, and His will must
be done. The one was refined and cultured, knew
the arts and sciences and was proficient in the art of
government and higher civilization. The other was
ignorant, and knew but little of his God. With this
difference in the two, one must be master, the other
must be slave. No criticisms nor unkind words are
necessary in such a masterpiece of work. It was God's
way and His ways are past finding out. The Negro
must be made a man, a Christian, a gentleman, and
a citizen. Ten million rough stones—chiseled into
marble statues. This was the white man's task, a
proclamation, and edict signed by God himself. Had
the white man known his task, had God revealed
unto him his duty in this mighty work, he would
have proclaimed his weakness and inability to perform it. Over the ruffled sea of time, and amid the
billows of thought, must this work be accomplished.
Tranquility, peace and harmony were not the attributes to be acquired or retained by the white man
of America. But, they must think differently, and
finally divide among themselves.

The Negro during this time must be taught to love, honor and obey. He must fight the battles of his country, he must uphold the flag of his country. He must know that the white man's God was his God, their country must be his country, and where they died he must die also. The Negro must submit to civilization, the rough corners of his conscience must be made smooth, his sensibilities must be sharpened, resentment made perceptible, and his very symmetry made more God-like. He must be taught the value of labor as to health and physical culture. The white man must teach him to be carpenters, brickmasons, shoemakers, dressmakers, laundrymen, in fact all the trades and artifices of civilization. Beneath the heat of a burning sun, an the zigzag lightning of the fiercest storm he must make the cotton and corn. The sweet melodies of the plantation song, beneath the rafters of the old log hut must bring him joy.

The Negro must not stop at cotton and corn, but during his two hundred and fifty years of bondage he learned to build cities, and railroads; he cleared the forest and what was once a dismal swamp, the miasma lands of the Mississippi Valley, he changed into the most valuable and productive field of all the world. He makes cotton king, and with his hand and labor, clothes and feeds all America. Previous to his emancipation he made a dependent of his master, and raised the pecuniary price of himself. He became the most valuable of all animal kingdom. He imbibed the white man's civilization, he learned and practiced his ways; and, as time rolled by he became more like the white man every day. The white man was his teacher;

he was an apt pupil. He taught him to work, and
he taught him to play; he taught him to preach, and
he taught him to pray; he taught him to steal, and
he taught him to fight; he taught him to read and he
taught him to write.

When the picture is properly drawn, our South-
land was a vast schoolroom filled with many valuable
teachers. Each teacher eager for as many pupils as
he or she could get. The Negro is greatly indebted
to the Southern white man for his civilization, his
refinement, his religion, and his industrial training.
The Negro's gratitude to him should be everlasting,
his love unbounded, and a perpetual treaty of peace
should be signed by both. It should be sealed with
the wax of love, and never opened except by kindness, patience and forbearance.

Under the burden of oppression the Negro grew
physically strong. Truth and vivacity played a
most prominent part in his character. I have been
told by many of the old ex-slaves, that one of the
most frequent texts chosen before the war was,
"Thou must not tell a lie. If you do you are in
danger of a hell that burns with brimstone and
fire." Truth was the one great moral lesson daily
taught him. Absolute confidence in all he should say
made him a most valuable Negro to his master. It
made it much easier for his master to control him,
while it made the Negro a much better man or
woman. It saved time and trouble for both. It
gave the Negro liberty, and the white man confidence.
It cleared conscience and broadened thought, and in
the end gave him a home beyond this vale of tears.
A perfect submission on the part of the Negro was

absolutely essential to his proper training and civilization. It was a part of God's plan to fit him for
freedom and citizenship. The rough corners of his
life must be knocked off, the faster the knocking, the
nearer he approached freedom. The harder the burden, the greater the division among the white man
as to the justice and right of slavery in free America.
The Mason and Dixon line, the under-ground railroad, the Missouri Compromise, the Kansas border
warfare, then a Wendall Phillipps, a William Lloyd
Garrison, all were but signals of an approaching end
of the first part of a mighty plan of God's to civilize,
and make citizens of ten million people. No mistakes or errors were made by either North or South,
in civilizing and working out the plans of salvation
and preservation of the Negroes of America.

I cannot share the doctrine of good Northern white
men, and mean Southern white men. I am a firm be-
liever in the wisdom of a great God. Both did their
duty, and if credit must be given for the advancement in civilization, in culture, and trades it certainly should be given the instructors.

The Indian has been a free man all his life, his
liberty was unrestrained. He has gone where he
pleased, worked when he pleased and worshiped the
God of his choice. He was here before the white man,
here before the Negro, but he has gone with the
forest, fallen with the grass and is fast passing out
beneath the stars and stripes. His God was not the
white man's God, his civilization not the white man's,
his country was his own, and in consequence he has
perished and died as the cattle upon a thousand hills.
His persistent efforts to shun civilization, to worship

the sun, moon and stars, rather than the great God
of love and obedience. His refusal to make his own
bread by the sweat of his brow, his fondest wish to
roam the forest and live as the beasts of the field,
was in direct opposition to Negro characteristics.   It
brought him woe, it brought him sorrow and will
bring him ultimate extermination.   What was once
his happy hunting grounds is transformed into fields
of cotton, corn and wheat.   His Indian village may
be called St. Louis, Chicago or New York.   His
numerical strength has sunk to a nonentity, and his
identity almost lost to sight.   But, the Negro as a
slave grew in numbers, grew in strength and civilization.

A comparison of the two races should convince the
most skeptical of the great advantage gained by the
Negro's perfect submission to the art of civilization.
Up to 1863 much blood had been shed, many lives
lost, and a billion dollars spent, all by white men
as to the rights and status of the American Negro.
But, in all the various Legislatures of the various
States of the Union, in the Congress of the United
States there was not one Negro to plead the cause of
his people, but his friends were legion.   Negro slavery
was the act of white men, his civilization was their
teaching, and his freedom their proclamation.

The entire program was made by the white man,
he made it as he pleased.   The Negro had no part
to play, except to learn, labor and to wait.   He was
an obedient servant, a hard worker, and an apt
scholar.   Hence no blame can be attached to him.
He is the innocent recipient of the white man's quarrels, his civilization and freedom.   His freedom in

1863 brought with it nothing but liberty. The foxes had holes, and the birds had nests, but the Negro had nowhere to lay his head, and call his own. But, with the gentleness of a child, with the love of a God, he returns to his former master's field there to work out his own as well as his former master's salvation. Impoverished and devastated by war, humble and poor we be, says old master, Come unto me all ye that are ladened and I will do my best. It is here the olive branch of peace was sung on the outer wall, and the voice of God, "Do unto others as you would have them do to you," was most prominently played both by the Southern white man and the Negro. It was here they startled the world with their mutual admiration and friendship, and it was here the capstone of a new South was laid.

AS A FREEMAN

Under the new order of things, that same old cornfield blooms with its tassels of gray; that same old cotton field stretches its snowlike bed through all the land and the sweet melody of the old plantation song sends joy and jubilation to every heart. The church bell is heard on every hill, the school bell in every dell. The new South arises from its slumber and becomes master of the situation, with two people, two distinct races, they are slowly but surely working out their own salvation. The new South was born with a new white man, with new thoughts and new ideas. He finds the Negro ignorant, his former master wearied, worn and terrified. The situation afforded an easy prey for graft. Just what was done during those days of resurrection is a question to be debated by the white men themselves. No sane man can justly charge anything to the Negroes' account. If the laws were good or bad it was not his fault; if legislation in the Southern States was wise and wholesome, the credit side of the white man's account must go up; if bad and mischievous, it must go down. The Negro is an "innocent accident" of the white man's quarrels. The Negro made no war, he declared no peace. His greatest blessing, that of liberty, was the gift of God, and the white man. With nearly one hundred per cent of ignorance in 1863, has the Negro advanced, or decreased that per cent to such a degree, that the nation can see a ray of hope for the further expenditure of millions of dollars for his education, refinement and ultimately his permanent citizenship? Our last census gave him a total gain of 55 per cent. Is there any outward showing of this decrease in ignorance among the Negroes is another question of special interest. I believe there is—it can be plainly seen in the thousands of schools. Teachers of his own race filling positions once held by white teachers. Twenty-five years ago it was a very rare thing to see a colored man or woman teaching and instructing the youth of their own race, but today it is just the reverse. It is almost a curiosity to see a white person instructing and teaching the Negro youths of the South. We have Negro school teachers with first-grade licenses by the thousands, but a little higher up the ladder and you will find Negro principals with two to twenty teachers under his supervision in any Southern city of any size or importance.

At the top of the ladder you will find Negro presidents of colleges, academies, and institutions of learning. These schools, colleges and institutions stand forth as living monuments of a marked advancement made by the Negroes of America.

Lavish sums of money have been given by States, and the generous philanthropists both North and South to maintain and properly equip these schools for the proper training into good citizens the Negro boys and girls of the country. I read through the columns of the press of the country only a few months ago where Mr. Carnegie appropriated $600,-000.00 to aid the work being done at Tuskegee.

May God, the great Ruler of the Universe, bless and preserve Mr. Carnegie, even to the end of time, and may others emulate his example and supplement his gift by a hundred fold. Until ignorance and superstition shall be entirely dethroned by morality, honesty, refinement and a thorough classical education for the classes, and complete industrial training for the masses.

We must have our doctors, lawyers, scientists and artists, but they are few compared with our need for farmers, carpenters, brickmasons, shoemakers, printers, painters, dressmakers and the like; a school that teaches the hand, head and heart to work in unison for the preservation and uplifting of the race. The turning of the soil, and making a good crop of corn, potatoes or cotton is a great art. It adds thousands of dollars of wealth to the country every year. Our cotton crop alone adds millions of dollars, gives employment to thousands of working people

in the South.   It turns all the spindles of the New
England States, and thereby makes bread for thousands of its citizens.   It, together with wool, clothes
the world, and gives comfort to all the earth.   The
Negro is the master hand in this great industry.
Should his hands refuse to work, his cotton fail to
grow, untold misery to all the world would be the
result.   It would shut down every gin in the United
States, close every spindle in the land, lock every
store door in the country, and spread desolation
throughout the world.   But, the Negro is the master
mechanic and he will order no boycott, no strikes,
either sympathetic or otherwise.   The hand must
work, the cotton must grow, the spindles must turn
and the people made happy, prosperous and rich by
the sweat of his brow.

Instead of idle hands, Tuskegee must make them
more scientific; for one good industrious farmer is
worth more to a community than one hundred gen-
teel dudes.   Your brickmasons, carpenters and other
tradesmen are as important in developing the wealth
and growth of our country as the farmer, for it was
their strong arm, muscle and brawn that laid waste
the forest, and built the cities, towns and villages
from the shores of Maine, to the Golden Gate of
California, and from the white snowclad hills of
Canada to the orange blossom fields of Florida.   A
first-class tradesman is always in demand, either at
home or abroad; a good tradesman carries the worth
of himself in his own hands.   It's found in the saw,
the hammer, and the square.   He can make his own
contract, set his own price, and be his own director;
in other words he is lord of all he surveys.

J. W. GOLDEN
State Grand Master of Indiana.

Born December 28, 1873, in Knox County, Ky.

Elected at the Indiana State Grand Lodge held at Gary, Ind., June 1-2, 1922. Re-elected September 12, 1923.

Seven lodges in the State when elected.

274 members in the State when elected.

Eleven lodges in the State at present, with 961 members.

Connected with the Order since July, 1916.

H. S. DAVIS
State Grand Master of Louisiana.

Born September 15, 1877, in Warren County N. C.

Elected at Grand Lodge session in July, 1915, at Shreveport, La.

Approximate number of lodges in the State when elected, 40.

Approximate number of members in the State when elected, 1,900.

Present number of lodges in the State, 390.

Present number of members in the State, 14,000.

Connected with the Order for eight and a half years.

It will be through the honest farmer, the skilled mechanic and the professional man that the Negro must work out his own salvation, and solve his own problem.

The dudes, loafers nor the poltroons of the race can neither solve it or assist others in doing so.

As graduates of Tuskegee let me entreat you to go forth into the world emulating the example of your distinguished president. Be men and women of iron will; at all times and under most adverse circumstances, dare to do right. If hatred for your fellow men lurks within your breast, curb it with a will of love; frown down, by precept and example, every spectacle of disloyalty; uphold and defend the majesty of the law; let each for one, and one for all, make the very best citizen in his or her community.

Let the world be better for your living in it; cultivate and encourage a friendly relation with your neighbor, be he black or white; practice and teach economy, friendship, love and truth. Save your earnings, buy lands, get homes, be as wise as serpents and harmless as doves.

This course pursued, will strengthen the bonds of friendship, sustain relationship and solve mathematically all problems, the race problems included.

In speaking of the economic side of the Negro problem, the New York Independent says: "The new economic development is about to put a new pressure upon the Negro race far more severe than any it has heretofore experienced." No intelligent student of industrial progress can fail to see that a considerable portion of the black race in the South is doomed. Under the new conditions that portion of the race will alone survive which is capable of mastering new industrial methods, and subjecting itself to the requirements of systematic, intelligent, faithful activity. Like every section of the country, the South is witnessing the concentration of capital. To a great extent the undertakers of the new Southern enterprises are Northern men and to a great extent the capital they control is Northern capital, and when the Northern business man finds Negro labor inefficient he does not hesitate for a moment to turn the Negro adrift, and give his position to a white man. To meet the conditions here quoted is the aim and object of industrial education. The Southern white man is much more lenient with your industrial faults than the Northern white man, but the Southern white man will some day grow impatient if the Negro, himself, does not keep up with the standard of requirements. The Southern white man prefers the Negro laborer, and in most instances will give him the preference over his own race. To retain this economic preference he must meet with all the requirements in all the trades and various callings. Not one inch of ground must be lost. If he is to build a house, he must build it better than anyone else, and according to architectural plans. If he is to launder clothes, it must be done as well or better than any one else. He must make more and better cotton on less land than is required by any one else. To do this he must have a thorough industrial training. The industrial field of the South at present belongs to the Negro. But to retain it, he must prepare himself for the sharpest competition. The white man of the South is his friend, and stands ready and willing to assist him in this preparation. The work is here to be done, and must and will be done, and that too, in the most competent and scientific way. A man's worth to his community is, in a large measure, judged by his industrial traits. No community is willing to dispose of its good, industrial farmers; villages, towns and cities are loathe to give up their skilled mechanics, brickmasons, etc., but the indolent, idle hand can always receive a willing "good bye", with a hope they may never return.

Industrial education is by far one of the most important subjects now before the American people. This subject is especially important to the Negro. Labor, both skilled and unskilled, like capital both great and small, forms a unit value in the government of a people. Both stand for something, and in the calculation of human affairs, both must be reckoned. No leader of a people can be safe and sound, unless he takes in account a proper provision, whereby the laborers of the race can get the most for his labor. To do this, he must prepare them in such a way as to be able to combat with the strongest competition.

In this connection, Tuskegee is doing her share of the work. The work and influence of Tuskegee are being felt in the schoolroom, in the workshop, on the housetop and on the farm. And, if my judgement has not led me astray, it is playing the master part in the solution of the Negro economic, if not his race question. The Negro has made rapid progress in preparing himself as a useful citizen since emancipation. It might be well to inform those who do not recognize his progress to here give a few figures of his wealth in trades and occupation. We have 51

colleges and institutions of high repute, and I believe
Tuskegee stands at the head of the list, all being well
attended by members of the race.   The common
school system is being well attended with something
like 1,200,000 youths in daily attendance, with about
thirty seven thousand teachers to instruct them. We
have 1,200 lawyers practicing in the various courts
of the country.   There are 1,100 medical doctors and
surgeons, all well patronized, and giving perfect satisfaction.   Some of this number making more than
$10,000 annually.   There are 130 dentists, there are
75 Negro drug stores, owned and operated by trained
pharmacists.   There are 25,000 colored boys and
girls, annually learning the various trades, thereby
moulding themselves into most useful citizens.

The Negroes own $850,000,000 worth of real
and presonal property.   There are 275,000 Negroes
that own farms, and devote their time to farming.

There are 1,800 colored men employed in the
Pullman service, there are police officers, 200,000 are
employed in the bar business, 500,000 who have
trades of various kinds.   There are 50,000 colored
people in business of one kind or the other.   There
are 2,500 mail carriers in the United States Post Office Department.   The colored people are publishing
1,000 newspapers and magazines, more than 350
books have been written and published by Negro
authors.   The blacksmith business has 6,500 colored
men who are practical smiths by trade.   In the Under-
taker and Enbalming business there are 1,400 colored
people, 4,000 are first class stenographers, 1325 are
telegraph operators, also 326 colored women are
telegraph operators, 7,496 first class engineers, 125,-

000 skilled miners, 2,400 colored men are carriage and wagon makers by trade, two thousand plumbers and gas fitters by trade, 325 inventors of patents, 125 clock and watch makers, 2,601 colored people in the United States raising tobacco, 22,000 are cigar makers by trade, 46,000 stone and brick masons by trade, 50,000 colored mechanics, 21,453 colored women are dressmakers by trade, 6,519 women who are highly educated in music, some are teaching music, 10,216 colored shoemakers. The Negroes have no suicides, and but few beggars. The tramp is one unknown quantity among the Negroes. These figures if carefully studied will remove some doubt from the most skeptical mind as to the Negro, and his worth to the nation as a citizen.

I congratulate the graduates of Tuskegee in making a choice so wise as this school.

Note: The figures quoted were taken from the census of 1900.

Service was Mr. Bush's "Shibboleth."   He rendered service to the members of his own family, his race and his country from his early manhood, and though through practicing thrift and frugality he had acquired a comfortable fortune and could have easily retired and take the comforts of life, he was on the firing line of his race's interest to the time of his death.

In 1905, a wave of agitation swept through the Southern States advocating the segregation of taxes for school purposes. This wave struck Arkansas and a bill was introduced in the State Legislature providing for this segregation. The bill had reached its third reading and the friends of Negro education were greatly alarmed. Mr. Bush at once threw all of his powerful influence into the fight. He personally saw influential white persons; wrote letters to others and almost in a night worked out formidable opposition to this iniquitous measure. The result was that the measure was defeated in a Democratic Legislature.

He addressed the following open letter to the members of the legislature and caused a change of opinion of many who had promised to support the measure. We publish the letter as it appeared in the Arkansas Gazette:

AGAINST SEGREGATION

J. E. Bush Makes Appeal to the General Assembly.
Little Rock, Arkansas, January 14, 1905.

To the Senators and Representatives of the General
Assembly of Arkansas:

Gentlemen: Before you cast your vote to segre-
gate the school taxes of our great and growing State,
so as to give the Negroes such school facilities as can
be provided by the taxes that he himself pays into
the treasury, I take this method of asking you why
discriminate against the great producing masses of our
State? Arkansas has a Negro population of about
334,000. This Negro population pays taxes on
$15,000,000.00 worth of real and personal property,
and, according to the report of the Auditor of State,
pays annually into the treasury about $250,000.00.
This is outside of the fines assessed against him by the
various courts of the State, which also constitute a
part of our school fund, and of this vast sum of
money paid annually he receives little or no benefit
except that of his free schools. He pays ungrudgingly
to maintain an ex-Confederate Home, pension to ex-
Confederates, their widows and orphans; he helps to
pay the salary of our good Governor and all other
State and county officers, and, I am sorry to say, he
is the mainstay of our constabulary force of the State;
and, in fact, he is the great storehouse of all your
wealth.

He has worked, toiled and enriched you and yours
for more than two hundred and fifty years and he
is still doing the same thing. I hope you have not
forgotten how our mothers and fathers tenderly

cared for you and yours while your strong sires were off at war. Have you forgotten that it was his strong arm and muscle that felled the trees, cleared the forest, built the cities and railroads for you? Don't you know that cotton is king, and the Negro the great producer thereof and you the greatest beneficiary therefrom. The estimated value of the world's annual output of cotton goods is $2,000,000,000.00. Three-fourths of all the world's cotton supply is grown in the Southern States of the United States. Twice the amount of gold produced last year would have been required to pay the Southern farmers and planters for lint and seed; three-fourths of the capital stock of all the banks in this country would have been inadequate. Our export cotton crop for 1903 was valued at $350,000,000.00, and 1904 will make a better showing. Take all other animal and vegetable products exported any year—wheat, corn, barley, oats, rye, flour, meal, oatmeal, fruits, vegetables, liquors, tobaccos, wines, cattle, sheep, beef, pork, mutton, butter, cheese, canned goods, lard, oils, wool, timber, lumber, naval stores, etc. Take this entire contribution from Maine to California, and from the Lakes to the Gulf of Mexico, and one year's cotton and cotton seed exports, the Southern cotton grower could buy the whole colossal aggregation and still have a surplus of $1,000,000.00 left him.

The Negroes are the fellows who produce this result for the Southern white man, and is this not sufficient in itself to guarantee his free schools? Is he not producing the wealth that you might pay, not only your own taxes, but his as well? Are you willing that he shall remain on the farms of Arkansas and enjoy the benefits of educating his children, or do you wish to drive him away and allow these farms to go to waste? These questions not only affect the farmer, but every railroad, business and professional man as well.

Gentlemen, voicing the sentiment of my people as I do, in the name of God, justice and right, I beg of you not to pass the segregation bill.

Yours for justice,

J. E. BUSH.

Mr. Bush was a keen student of the economic conditions affecting his race and took an active part in every movement or organization that had to do with this particular phase of the question. He was among the charter members of the National Negro Business Men's League which was founded by the late Dr. Booker T. Washington. He served in various capacities from the organization of the league up to his death. For years he was on the very important National Executive Committee of the league.

It was through his personal effort that one of the annual sessions of this organization was held in Little Rock. This meeting brought to the State the most representative group of colored men in the nation and was of untold good in removing many false impressions concerning Arkansas.   For years Arkansas had suffered from the ridicule of jokesmiths and to some extent the general public had come to believe in a way that these jokes were true.   Mr. Bush seized this opportunity to place the State which he loved so well in its proper light and in this effort he was ably seconded by the representative white citizens of the State.   The Governor and the mayor of the city welcomed the league and the business interests of the city contributed their full share in making the meeting a success.   It is probable that no other man in Little Rock could have secured such hearty co-operation from every source as did Mr. Bush.

At the annual meeting of the league in Louisville Mr. Bush delivered one of the principal addresses and by reason of his independent attitude on any position that he might take, this address provoked nation-wide discussion.   He stood by his guns during the round of criticism from certain forces at variance with Mr. Washington's theories but time and recent developments have justified his wisdom.

His speech at the Business Men's League of the State of Mississippi represents his attitude to the economic position occupied by the race. He spoke as follows:

Mr. President, Delegates, Ladies and Gentlemen:

I deem this an interesting occasion, and an honor to have been invited to address you. The assembling of delegates and visitors to the Negro Business Men's League here, is a compliment that this city should be proud of. The history of this organization in your State is yet unknown, but its splendid membership should be a full guaranty of its future good to all the people of your State. It derived its name from a similar organization of national repute, and if the child should be likened unto its father, you have need to rejoice. Of all organizations, secret or otherwise, none has had such a stimulating effect, with greater actual results, than the National Negro Business Men's League, of which Booker T. Washington is president, and I take it for granted, that this organization, the Negro Business Men's League of Mississippi, will follow in the path already marked out by its sire. If this shall be done, we will all say, "Well done, thou good and faithful servant of a most grateful people". As business men, your motto should be "Industry"—it is the brightest beacon light of mankind; it should be the foundation rock of every member of your organization.

The All-Wise Being has seen proper to create no two persons exactly alike, no two leaves in the forest similar in all their parts, no two things in nature the precise counterpart of the other—as our physical forms are different, so are our mental attributes, personal character, ambition and business tact. Every man or woman that may start in business will not succeed just like his brother, but if you are imbued with the true spirit of industry, morality and fair dealing, your success is assured, if not, you might as well write your prospects of success upon the running waters. Forget not this rule—"Take care of the moments and the hours will take care of themselves. Multiply and save your dimes and your dollars are made." Remember this above all, "To thine own self be true and it will follow as the night the day, thou canst not then be false to any man."

We have much to be proud of as ex-slaves and their descendants, and much more should we rejoice as being American citizens. As ex-slaves, we were honest, faithful, trustworthy and hard workers—our chief aim being to please our owners and give general satisfaction at whatever our hands found to do. No claim of false pride or betrayal of trust was ever charged to our account, but we were always delighted when the sun shone the brightest, and when peace and contentment reigned supreme around the capitol of our old plantation home. Our owners' sorrows were our sorrows—when they wept—we wept with them, and their happiness was our greatest joy. As citizens we should practice both by precept and example, the same principle now. We have made rapid strides as home-getters and money-savers since our emancipation, and we have also greatly reduced our illiteracy. As home-getters, we have startled the world, and excited most favorable comment from the unbiased thinker and writer of today.

In giving the wealth in farms and farming products, the census enumerators give the following facts which should be very gratifying to ourselves and friends. (Here the speaker recited a number of statistics showing the remarkable progress of the race.)

The figures here given apply only to farms, but it goes without saying that his personal and realty values in the towns and cities are even more startling. In the city of Little Rock, Arkansas, he pays taxes on more than $1,000,000.00 worth of real and personal property, and when you are told that all property in Arkansas is assessed at 60 per cent of its real value, you will then see that the Negroes of Little Rock, Arkansas, own $1,600,000.00 in real and personal property. In this connection I am pleased to state that Little Rock does not stand alone in this respect—there are others, and I hope that this city is among the number. With the same ratio of increase in getting farms—within 120 years, the Negroes will own and operate every farm in the Southern States. This is no wild speculation, but a cold, mathematical fact, receiving its answer from a careful examination of what has already been done. The Negro business man is yet a youth, and every phase of his future can only be considered problematically. It is true, however, that we have many

scattered evidences here and there, of his ability to
achieve success.   In business as in everything else, he
must take his lessons from those around him.   You
must know that from every calling, from all the ranks
of business and labor, mercantile, professional and
mechanical, that yearning cry is heard, marking steady
diffusion of intelligence, enlarged appreciation of the
power of knowledge, increased numbers, set free in
intellect by their free equality in law.   The lamp of
science now bestows its rays on every scene of human
efforts, and the quickening power of its light stim-
ulates inquiry and growth, and everywhere industry
adds some product for the comfort and joy of man.
The teeming mouth of the mine is vocal with the
sound of inventive science; the forest in rapid fall,
reverberates its mighty stroke; the farmside mingles
the melody of civilization's machinery with nature's
voices, and in various forms the manufactory hums
the note of enlightened progress.   New methods constantly grant greater forces to man, multiply the old
and develop new products to enter the marts of trade.

The business man is the agent and factor of all
the ranks of industry and life; gathering from every
class, distributing to every class.   He must be quick
to know the wants of all, the availability of the
products of all.   At his highest value, he must ad-
vantageously partake of the knowledge of all.   His
intelligence must comprehend not only the necessities,
but the luxuries, delicate tastes and gratification of
all.   He must teach the producer the demands of
society, the consumer, the richest fruits of labor.   So
great are the demands on the business man that the
American people will not allow him to limit his

efforts in his own country. He has ever been and forever will be, the adventurous trader of the globe, and now, more than ever, for thousands of avenues are opening every day, and new fields are inviting his attention, where but a few years ago only a small field challenged his attempt. The railroads and steamboats have made all the produce of earth his commodities; every clime his garden; every people his customer. His eyes must be ever open, and his ear must catch the notes of daily traffic. His factors are in Europe, Asia, Africa, and the far isles of the sea, and his competition oustrips his rivals in every land and every clime. He must be alert, enterprising and bold, such is the character and mission of a successful and great business man. Whosoever is unwilling to undergo the conditions here outlined, must take in contentment his lesser place.

The highest rank in any calling can be reached only by possession of the gifts and acquirements requisite to perform its function, and the noblest aim and effort lead honorably to the foremost place, those of you who would look to be leaders in your business, must hold out the greatest inducement to your customers. You must buy the best at the least reasonable cost, let your selling price at all times be measured by the cost, thus giving your customers the advantage of your business tact, both in cost and profits. Business men sometimes mistake wild speculation as the nearest cut to riches, they undertake to make short cuts across, lose their better judgment, and the result is bankruptcy, disgrace and ruin. I would advise against "get-rich-quick" schemes, futures and the like. Much of the future advancement of the race

depends upon your untiring efforts to succeed.   Our
schools, colleges and academies are turning out about
5,000 graduates each year, and these graduates must
find a field of labor, our professors and teachers find
their source of livelihood already overcrowded—our
pulpits are much in the same fix.   Supply and demand are the regulators in prices and salaries, hence
we often hear the remark, "Poor pay, poor preach."
Our business men must be depended upon to relieve
this congestion or condition of affairs.   We must
have banks, factories, grocery stores, both wholesale
and retail, shoe stores and in the near future, operate
railroads, steamboats and telegraph and telephone
lines, thus opening new avenues for the employment
of this intelligent surplus supply.   This can only
be successfully done by a united effort of all concerned.

   This is the lesson aimed to be taught by the National Negro Business Men's League, and the cardinal
principles that actuated your meeting in this State.
It was the business men who discovered the brotherhood of man, and pioneered the civilization which
Christianity purified.   It was the business man who
caused the ships to plow the mighty ocean and made
the whole world kin.   It was the business man who
built the railroad, tunnelled the mountain and tied
our cities with brotherly love.   It was the business
man who chained the lightning, built telegraph and
telephone lines, and made the "hello girl", and as we
stand here tonight in the mere youth-time of our existence, may we not strain a prophetic eye to a future
day when the American Negro Business Men may
cause the great arteries of trade to burst forth with

such splendor as to afford employment to the 5,000 boys and girls that our schools and colleges are giving annually.

In later years Mr. Bush was much in demand as a speaker on various occasions within and without the State and being of an obliging disposition found it hard to refuse. This laid a heavy burden on him, for the rapid expansion of the Order had made his duties manifold.

He insisted as long as his physical condition would permit, on having personal oversight of every detail of the office work. He was particularly interested in every complaint that came into the office, regardless of how trivial it might be, he always personally replied in courteous terms and found opportunity to express interest in the personal welfare of the writer. This attitude greatly endeared him to the thousands of the members of the Order of more humble station and they came to look upon him as a sort of big brother. When his health began to fail and his physician had forbid him to longer climb the stairs to the main office, he insisted on being carried down in his car to the office building and there in a buggy, drawn by a little pony, the property of his nephew, and to which he was fondly attached notwithstanding that he had his own autos he practically opened office in this buggy and continued in this way personal contact with the office, depending largely on his younger son, A. E. Bush to see that his orders were carried out.

His wearing down became apparent to his intimate friends and close associates and finally yielding to their entreaties he gave up attention to the office and spent the remainder of the few months that were left to him in the companionship of his friends, many of whom were men of very humble station. His greatest joy was his opportunity to sit down and listen to these "children of the sun" relate their quaint jokes and experiences.

We make no effort to give the details of his death and funeral. This was so beautifully and faithfully told in the eulogy delivered by Mr. John Hamilton McConico at the

National Grand Lodge meeting which was held in Little Rock in the year 1917. We give the address in full, not only for its historical value but for its literary excellence.

Mr. McConico's relation as a national officer in the Mosaic Templars of America brought him into close contact with Mr. Bush and no man save the immediate members of his family had better opportunity for close association than had Mr. McConico:

AN EULOGY BY JOHN HAMILTON McCONICO

Representing the Twelfth Triennial Session Mosaic Templars of America, July 11, 1917, Little Rock, Arkansas.

To the Officers and Delegates of the National Grand Lodge—*Greetings*:

Today is the close of an epoch in Mosaic history. The central figure in the thirty-three years just closed has gone the way of all the earth and we have assembled here to give fitting recognition to the close of a "Perfect Day." We have assembled with the fond hope that tomorrow's sun will rise not only upon a new day, but upon a day whose sun will set upon a morning, a noonday and an evening that has been filled with honest effort, noble purpose and glorious achievement in the battle for the betterment of man.

When the late C. W. Keatts, one of our founders and our first National Grand Master, departed this life—the National Committee of Management selected me to deliver the eulogy. In July, 1913, the successor of C. W. Keatts, William Alexander, requested me to deliver his eulogy whenever death should call him. Almost in a spirit of levity I agreed, little thinking that four months later I would stand over his lifeless form—his work brought to an abrupt close by the hand of an assassin. Some months ago, the subject of our eulogy today, J. E. Bush, said to me, "Well, if you survive me, present my life's work to the Mosaic Templars of America just as you did Messrs. Keatts' and Alexander's." Grateful to Almighty God, I am here thankful that I have been spared to carry out my part of the agreement. You are here as National Grand Lodge to pay tribute to our departed founder and National Grand Secretary. Mark not this occasion with lamentation and sorrow. Let every heart be light and every soul happy that the life recently closed was lived so well, filled with so much usefulness, and left such a priceless heritage to us all.

Love is a stronger passion than hate and those for whom we live will love us, admire our accomplishments and honor, revere and keep alive our memories. Therefore it is one of the lasting credits of our civilization that the "Flowers born to blush unseen and waste their fragrance on the desert air" are rare exceptions to the general rule. The life that is devoted to noble, honest and unselfish endeavor, stamps its impress indelibly upon the human heart and instead of fading away with the passing of years, on the other hand, as decades glide into eternity, the lustre grows brighter.

W. T. RADFORD

State Grand Master of Michigan.

Born August 22, 1879, in Calhoun County, Ala.

Elected State Grand Master June 15, 1921, at Grand Lodge held at Detroit, Mich.

Approximate number of lodges in the State when elected, 11.

Present number of lodges in the State, 23.

Connected with the Order for 12 years.

W. H. FERRELL

State Grand Master of Georgia.

Born June 15, 1872, in Nelson County, Va.

Appointed State Grand Master for the State of Pennsylvania in 1919, serving until late 1920. Appointed State Grand Master of Georgia in 1924, succeeding R. G. Elliott, who resigned on account of failing health.

Approximate number of members when elected, 700.

Present number of members, 1,000.

Connected with the Order for 8 years.

In line with the above sentiments, we have assembled here to pay fitting homage to the life and
services of John Edward Bush, the founder of the
Mosaic Templars, and ever ready champion of the
Negro race.   There was an intimacy of relationship
existing between the deceased and myself that will
cause the personal pronoun "I" to make frequent
appearance in this effort—for which I solicit if not
your patience, your tolerance.   It would be a useless
waste of time to attempt to narrate in detail the life
and service of John Edward Bush.   His history is
written in the permanent literature of his time and
upon the hearts of his fellow men.   The date of his
birth would have no special significance or bearing
had he not been born a slave.   To you it matters little
when he was born, to the world it matters little now
when he died—the one thing that will concern all
is how well he wrought while he was here.

GOOD OUT OF EVIL

John Edward Bush was a product of slavery and
bore its mark.   To mention slavery must cause re-
vulsion and horror in every Negro's heart.   Yet
slavery had its benefits as well as evils.   It gave to
the world many priceless heritages.   The struggle
for and against slavery developed a galaxy of mental
stars whose brilliancy has never been eclipsed.   It
produced a formidable array of military heroes who
will be idols of the human heart as long as mankind
admires genius and worships bravery.   Eliminate
Henry Clay, John C. Calhoun, Bob Tombs, Alexander Stephens, William Lloyd Garrison, Wendell
Phillips, Frederick Douglas, Stonewall Jackson, Rob-

ert E. Lee, Abraham Lincoln and Harriet Beecher
Stowe and Sojourner Truth and American history
must lose 50 per cent of its richness.

The ear of the world, speaking from a psychic
viewpoint, is deceptive, shy, modest and elusive.
Many, in its quest, have wound up with a wasted life
for their reward. Only the extraordinary characters
ever penetrate the hidden retreat and reach the ear of
the universe. The fact that J. E. Bush founded the
Mosaic Templars of America and reached the dizzy
heights of political fame—the fact that Booker T.
Washington founded Tuskegee and gave to the educational world the only new thought advanced in a
century, was and is not responsible, primarily for
their rise to greatness; but the fact that they came
from under slavery's yoke and in spite of its degrada-
tion, in spite of its humility, in spite of its suppres-
sion of manhood, in spite of its stagnation of mental
development, in spite of its annihilation of hope, in
spite of its destruction of aspiration, rose above it,
stamped under their feet, defied the prejudice and oppression of a race of a thousand years' advantage,
placed noble achievement to their credit and obligated
civilization and posterity to them. The majority of
the patriots who came to the crux of their fame and
usefulness out of the rise and fall of slavery have
long since pitched their tents upon fame's eternal
camping ground—they have crossed the silent river,
Washington and Bush with the rest, but their camp-
fires have been left burning and the light therefrom
will illuminate the pathway, attract as well as inspire
wayfaring pilgrims of many generations yet unborn.

OVERCOMING OBSTACLES

Soon after emancipation, J. E. Bush was brought to Little Rock by his mother and was soon left an orphan upon the streets of this city. Expressing it in his own language, he had no home and slept under bridges and in livery stables as often as he did in a house. He eked out an existence by doing chores such as carrying notes, watering stock, washing dishes, etc. In such a life there is a great lesson. John E. Bush was born in a hut and in a measure fed upon the husks of the swine, yet almost single-handed and unassisted he overcame his obstacles and died in a palace. Without friends and with meager educational opportunities, he overcame—then what should the young Negro do who is surrounded by schools, finds helping hands at every turn? His life has simply said to you, that if you will dedicate your life to the work you choose, that if you will go into the virgin forest and make the Marechal Niel grow from the stem of the primeval rose, that if you will make two ears of corn grow where one grew before, that if you will write a better book or sing a more beautiful song, though your hut may be located in the dense forest, the world will make a pathway to your door.

John E. Bush was what is commonly called a bad boy. Nothing else could have been expected. Col. R. C. Lacy, one of our pioneers who is now in the evening of life, delights to tell of picking him up one morning and stopping him from throwing rocks and carried him by main force to school. This was his first introduction to school and from the first he liked it. When he was unable to attend his classes

he kept up by studying at night, however, his deport-
ment in the community changed very little for the
better.   To give you an idea of how he stood, the
Sunday school of a certain church in this city was
giving a concert.   The audience had assembled and
the participants in the concert marched in and disappeared behind the curtains.   A certain prominent man
of this city when he saw little John Bush and Ches.
Keatts march behind the scenes with the other children, he immediately went forth and got his son
and daughter and informed the director that his
children could not appear on the same program with
two street rats like John and Ches.   His children
were the principals in the concert and as a result the
program was about ruined.   The years went by and
as they went misfortune overtook this man.   His
early holdings gradually vanished and the day came
that the John Bush despised and rejected in his youth,
held the hand of protection over this man's family
and placed bread in the mouths of his hungry children and he did it without once thinking of the little
episode that took place at the concert many years
before.

John E. Bush was not popular in Little Rock
during his early life.   The upward strides of no man
were more bitterly contested and opposed than were
those of John E. Bush in this city.   He courted and
married his wife under protest.   His wife came from
one of the oldest and most aristocratic families in
this city.   It was not believed that John E. Bush
would be able to provide for her, but she was the
judge and she decided that she saw something in
John E. Bush that others did not see.   Summing it

up in the language of an early enemy but a late friend,
"No matter what the hardships John Bush had to
encounter, Cora has never had to do anything but
sit on the front porch and rock."

After obtaining a pretty fair education he got a position in the Little Rock city schools, but the night he
married, his enemies had him put out of the schools.
Thus on the morning of his honeymoon he awoke
with no money, out of a job and nothing tangible
that he could see but a wife. Later he got in the
railway mail service and his oldtime enemies followed
him. For seventeen years they continued to hammer
on him and he finally had to leave the railway mail
service and start a newspaper as a weapon with which
to beat off his enemies. The "little Negroes" or
middle classes liked him, but the aristocracy despised
him. In spite of all these things he was an ardent
lover of his people and was ever ready with his
meager ability to do anything to advance their interests. He spent much time in studying the needs
and weaknesses of the race and often counseled with
his chum and co-worker, C. W. Keatts, as to what
were the best remedies. In 1883 the opportunity of
his life was forced upon him and he took the initiative
which was to later immortalize his name.

FOUNDING MOSAIC TEMPLARS

I have often stated to the members of the Order
that three distinct causes gave birth to the Mosaic
Templars of America: First, a white man's scorn;
second, a Negro woman's poverty; third a Negro's
shame. In 1883 a young Negro was standing on a
corner of the streets in Little Rock talking to a prom-

inent white man. While they talked an old Negro
woman came up and asked that they give her something to assist in burying her dead husband. Both
of the men helped her and as she left, the white man,
prefacing his remarks with an oath, said to the Negro:
"I cannot see or understand your race. When they
work they throw their earnings away and whenever a
Negro dies or needs help the public must be worried
to death by Negro beggars—it is a shame!" This
thrust stung the young Negro to the quick and he resolved upon the spot that if God would give him
the aid that he would lead out to remedy that condition in Little Rock. This man was none other than
John E. Bush. After counseling with his friend,
C. W. Keatts, they called together fifteen men and
women and organized the first Mosaic Templars
Lodge in the world. J. E. Bush and C. W. Keatts
sat on the steps of an old building that stood upon
this site and worked out the plans that brought into
existence the Mosaic Templars of America. They
started the organization as a home benevolent organization and never intended to operate outside of Little
Rock, but it only took a few years for the Order to
outgrow Little Rock, and the fondest hope of its
founders. The idea was too big to be hindered by
human hands. They started here with one lodge of
fifteen members, but today we have more than 2,000
lodges. We started here with fifteen members, but
today we have 80,000. We started here to remain
here, but we are now operating in twenty-six States,
Central America, Panama and the West Indies. We
started out to benefit only home people, but today
Negroes are wearing Mosaic pins. We know they

are Mosaics from the signs they make, but their language we speak not. The organization started out without sufficient funds to incorporate, but my brethren, John E. Bush so safeguarded the dimes entrusted to his care that today our net assets exceed $300,-000.00. John E. Bush so safeguarded your funds that in 1913 we bought the old site where he and Brother Keatts worked out the plans of the Order, razed the old shack to the ground and upon that sacred spot erected a magnificent structure of brick, steel, stone and mortar that is not only a credit to the Mosaic Templars of America, but a crowning achievement of the Negro people throughout the world.

John E. Bush was always an active and aggressive Republican politician, and after winning many minor victories reached his highest political attainment in 1900 by being appointed receiver of the United States land office, this city. As a sagacious and astute politician John E. Bush has few equals. This was evidenced during the administration of President Taft. He was the only Negro holding high Federal office, excepting in Washington, D. C., that survived the Taft weeding ax. Until his death a few years ago, General Powell Clayton, of reconstruction days, was the political boss of Arkansas and dispenser of Federal patronage. When Mr. Bush was quite a young man, General Clayton had him to go to a very dangerous community to make a political speech. When he returned, he wanted to pay him. Mr. Bush refused money and when General Clayton asked him if he wanted no money what did he want—he replied, your influence as long as you have any and as long

as I deserve it.   You have it, was the reply, and up
to the death of General Clayton the truce had not
been broken.

His appointment as receiver of the United States
land office for a second term came up under Roosevelt.   In entering high service of the Government Mr.
Bush's enemies had not despaired and they had deluged Roosevelt with so many charges against him
that Roosevelt refused to appoint him under recommendation of General Clayton, or the State Central
Committee of Arkansas.   The new President wanted
high-grade Negroes in office.   He knew little of the
Southern Negro of prominence other than Booker T.
Washington.   Mr. Roosevelt stated frankly that he
would only appoint him on recommendation from
Booker T. Washington.   Prof Booker was called
upon to go to Tuskegee and make an effort to get
Mr. Washington's support.   While Prof. Booker
knew Mr. Washington casually, he knew little of the
inner circle of Tuskegee.   At that time I was teaching at the Arkansas Baptist College, and knew much
about the manners and customs of Tuskegee, having
visited there several times as the representative of the
late W. H. Councill.   I knew Emmett Scott was the
man behind the throne at Tuskegee, and I advised
Prof. Booker to spend no time in searching for Booker
T. Washington, but bring Emmett Scott around to
his plans.   The trip to Tuskegee was made and Prof.
Booker returned with the endorsement of Booker
T. Washington speeding on its way to Washington,
D. C.   The appointment came and the following
summer Mr. Bush met Booker T. Washington at the

Business League in Nashville. It only took one day for Booker T. Washington to see that J. E. Bush was no ordinary man possessed of an ordinary mind. He immediately took him into his cabinet, made him his right hand lieutenant, and this place he retained until Booker T. Washington died.

The next time he came up for appointment, the State Central Committee decided that all of the white office-holders would be recommended for reappointment, but that J. E. Bush had held office long enough. They perfected plans for his slaughter. He instructed them not to present his name to the committee for recommendation. J. E. Bush, though they did not know it, was now bigger than a little bunch of men who met to dispense offices. The committee began to investigate, to find out the cause of his indifference. They found that J. E. Bush had visited Washington upon invitation of President Roosevelt, to discuss the welfare of the Republican party in the South and other matters affecting the Negro race; and while in Washington had been asked by the President if he wanted to take his commission of reappointment home with him or have him, the President, mail it to him later. The committee was panic stricken and hastened to recommend him in order to save their faces.

On the platform Mr. Bush was void of elegance, but abundant in force backed up with multitudes of facts. At the Business League in Atlanta, 1906, he proved his value to the race. On the night of the welcome exercises, the fact that Dr. Washington was to deliver his annual address had filled every available seat and standing space in Big Bethel Church.

The cream of the Negro race was there from all parts
of the world.   Press representatives from every large
daily in the South were there—some of them women.
It was just ten days prior to the Atlanta riots.   The
setting for the riot had then been made complete and
only needed the button pressed to put it in motion.
That night the program had almost been completed.
Dr. Washington had delivered a masterly address in
thought and timeliness. He was up making announcements for the next day's session.   Mr. T. Thomas
Fortune, the veteran editor of the New York Age,
got up and started toward the platform exit.   Some
one called for Fortune.   In a minute a thousand
throats were yelling Fortune.   Every Negro knows,
or should know, T. Thomas Fortune.   Great on
courage but mighty shy on judgment.   Mr. Washington very reluctantly called Mr. Fortune to the
front and introduced him.   Mr. Fortune already fired
by the abuse of Negroes in the Atlanta papers and
numerous insults inflicted upon delegates by street
car conductors and policemen, immediately assailed
the South and Southern white people.   In his tirade
of fury he fairly burned the atmosphere. He wound
up by charging the Southern white women with being the most unwomanly in all history as all the
trouble was about her and she stood and saw innocent
Negroes lynched without offering one word in their
defense.   They say there is no such thing in nature
as perfect silence.   There was silence that night in
Bethel Church.   The sage of Tuskegee had met his
Gethsemane.   The hour of trial was at hand.   His
hand was upon his breast.   He scanned the five hundred or more faces on the platform until his eyes

rested upon Mr. Bush. He called upon him to answer
Mr. Fortune. The old Mosaic hero came forth walk-
ing like some knight of the 16th century. His eyes
were sparkling until they resembled balls of fire and
his hair bristled like the mane about a lion's head.
His voice rang clear and strong. In an hour he had
annihilated Mr. Fortune, he had let the world know
that the Negroes of the South hated the bad white
people, but loved the good ones—he clearly demonstrated that the Business League was for the development of Negro business and not to agitate the race
question. He sat down from sheer exhaustion but
he had saved Booker T. Washington—he had saved
his race.

By 1908 J. E. Bush was mingling in that small
group of men that had been claimed by fame. His
oldtime enemies could not understand it for the reason
that he lived in a different world. They did not
know that the slave child from Tennessee forty years
before had dreamed dreams. They did not know
that in the dying embers of the evening fire, the vision
of his destiny had come before him. They did not
know that while driving wood wagons and off-bear-
ing bricks, that he was communing with the spiritual forces. In this manner he was taught lessons
of which the material mind can take no cognizance.
The laws governing the forces of nature taught him
the gospel of work. In all of nature there was the
divine plan of work. Just as soon as the tiny plant
unfolded its leaves it began to die. Stars, planets and
worlds were continually whirling in their orbits not
for a moment resting and the music of the solar system was so harmonious that it made no sound that

could be heard by finite ears—thus if there were this eternal harmony between life and work in the inanimate world, then why should the crowning event of Eden, the supreme effort of God seek rest. Gathering his inspiration from the stars, gathering his inspiration from the flowers, gathering hope and courage from the flowers, gathering hope and courage from those who came, who saw, who conquered, he set his feet in the path—Satan tempted him, drenching rains, blinding snows, and biting winds bore upon him, but he had turned his face toward Jerusalem, he had his eye fixed upon the morning star and his heart upon God and he could not fail.

IN THE SPOTLIGHT

During the last ten years of Mr. Bush's life he enjoyed in peace the laurels he had won. The greatness of it all was that he held no bitterness against his adversaries and failed not once to help them when he could. The culmination of his glory came in the dedication of this building. Great Negroes from all parts of the world had come to do him honor. Booker T. Washington was here to place upon his brow laurel wreath. His fame firmly established, he was standing in the high noon of his glory and he cast a shadow neither east nor west. The slave child, by strength of determination and giant will power had pulled himself from the muck and mire and now was a commanding figure among men. The boy born under the curse of slavery had overcome its taint, elbowed his way among the great men of earth and walked and talked with kings.

WM. J. MORSELL
State Grand Master of Illinois.

Born November 25, 1872, in Baltimore, Md.

Appointed State Grand Master of Illinois at the National Grand Lodge held at Little Rock, Ark., July, 1917.

Approximate number of lodges in the State when elected, 20.

Approximate number of members in the State when elected, 400.

Present number of lodges in the State, 33.

Present number of members in the State, 1,200.

Joined the Order January, 24, 1916.

A. W. WEATHERFORD
State Grand Master of Texas.

Born July 5, 1875, at Springfield, Ill.

Elected State Grand Master at the State Grand Lodge held at Sulphur Springs, Texas, July 12, 1913.

Approximate number of lodges in the State when elected, 26.

Approximate number of members in the State when elected, 600.

Present number of lodges in the State, 250.

Present number of members in the State, 6,000.

Connected with the Order for 18 years.

His increase in influence and prestige did not seem to exalt but humble him. He realized with such opulence of equipment as he possessed, there was necessarily coupled profound responsibilities. With his greatness was blended the truest type of goodness. It was his desire to have the sunshine of hope warm the hearts of those he touched and to plant flowers where thistles grew. From his every act radiated a beautiful belief in the power and purposes of the Savior of the world. He did not stop to inquire, he did not become confused as to whether there is a life beyond the grave, but accepted free from all doubt that a place had been prepared for him not built with hands. From study and experience his mind developed a hundred fold. He explored known and speculative science, dabbled into various schools of philosophy, yet to the day of his death he remained true to the spiritual inclinations of his race. To him Gethsemane's awful hour was not a brutal error, Calvary's tragic drama not a wanton waste and to him the resurrection was but typical of man's entry, after the storm of life is stilled into a day of eternal peace and fadeless glory.

HIS HOUSE IN ORDER

The business life of J. E. Bush was a revelation in its exactness. He kept his business in front of him, he never let it get where he could not see it. In prosecuting his life's work he had very little lost motion and the result was at 50 years of age he had more to his credit in achievement than the average man at 70. His whole life had been filled with hard work and as he went he put his house in order. Before he reached 60 years of age he had completed his work on earth.

His family, the ever present idols of his life, had been
guided by him to maturity. His daughter was married
and living happily. His two sons had come to noble
manhood and refused to allow the father to again
lay his hands to the plow. His wife who joined him
in his youth was standing by his side where she had
stood for over thirty years and was to him then the
same ministering angel she had been when the bloom
of youth was on her cheeks. His efforts for humanity
had placed his name in the archives of fame and recorded his memory in the hearts of men. The Mosaic
Templars which had stood next to his family in his
affections was now thoroughly established and was a
world-wide organization. The friends who had
helped him had been rewarded, the foes who had
fought him had repented. John E. Bush thus stood
as one of the few who really had realized every ideal
of his life, had accomplished the work he set out to
do. It was too late in life for him to lay out new
tasks, too late to undertake new ventures. During
1915 he was sitting in his office talking to National
Grand Master Elliott and myself. The question of
death came up. Without hesitation, Mr. Bush re-
marked that he cared absolutely nothing about death
and was ready and would go at any time without regret. I have made my mark, my family is provided
for, my friends are safe and I have brought the organization to the point now where it will run itself.
He gave evidence of no illness at that time, but I
told the Grand Master that Mr. Bush felt that his
mission was ended and I believed that he really
wanted to go. The death of Booker T. Washington
shocked him much and the various atrocities per-

petrated against Negroes throughout the country weighed upon him heavily. He brooded over these matters to the extent that he seriously considered removing our headquarters to the far west.

In February, 1916, he was stricken and never returned to his office again. He wanted to go then but his family and anxious friends pulled him from the deathbed and he came back to give us the benefit of his sunshine, he came back to encourage us a little with his presence. Through the spring, summer and fall he was with us. Relieved of all worry and work he did naught but ride over the beautiful hills that he had known since boyhood and sat and conversed with family and friends. December 9th, his oldest son, Chester, Grand Master Elliott and myself were in Memphis conducting district meetings. The summons came, "Come home." We found him surrounded by his family and friends. Nothing that human hands could do for him was missing. As he lived, he died. He met death without a shudder or frown. I stood at the foot of the bed and watched the life pass that had meant so much to my people. As I stood there I saw the little red-headed orphan boy sleeping in the gutters of Little Rock. I saw him scorned and despised by those of better estate. I saw him shaking off the chains that held him. I saw him holding in his hands commissions from four Presidents of the United States. I saw him battling for his race in Atlanta. I saw the air castle of his youth transformed into the Mosaic Templars of America. About me was sobbing and weeping, but it seemed that I could see the great white way opening from earth to heaven filled with angels waiting to bear home the fleeting spirit.   I felt like crying out, "Oh, death where is thy sting, oh, grave where is thy victory."   I said to the officials of the Order, dry your tears, prophecy has simply been fulfilled: "Ethiopia has stretched forth her hand to God, a Prince has come from Egypt."

He left his home in order.   His mantle fell upon his sons.   He owed no debts.   He had rendered unto Caesar the things that were Caesar's and the property of the organization was in perfect tact.   Every dime that he held of the Order's was in place.   For thirty years he had kept faith and when he died he knew that the organization had erected monuments over all of our deceased national officers of high rank, yet he provided for his monument to be built out of his estate.   The Mosaic Templars stepped in here and said no, that Bush lived and died for the Mosaic Templars.   His estate cannot build his monument. We are going to build it out of our hearts.   His monument when completed will be the property of the Mosaic Templars and the American people.   My friends, we are erecting in yonder city of the dead a house of stone for his earthly remains.   The records of the organization that he built shall be deposited with his remains.   His likeness shall be carved in marble and placed thereon and the record of his achievements placed in the tomb.   Centuries after you and I shall have passed, wayfaring pilgrims journeying this way will stop and read the inscription and they will know that on that spot fell a giant oak in the forest of men.

The following beautiful tribute to the life
and memory of Mr. Bush was delivered at
the National Grand Lodge meeting in Little
Rock by the Rev. J. W. Goodgame, prominent prelate of Birmingham, Alabama, and
who now holds the very high position of National Aaronic Master in the organization:

WHAT J. E. BUSH DID FOR HIS RACE

(Delivered by Rev. J. W. Goodgame, N. G. L.,
Birmingham, Ala.)

When a great earthly potentate, or an individual
distinguished for military prowess, or noted for ministerial gifts or remarkable civic ability, passes from
the stage of action, the whole civilized world is speedily apprised of its loss.   The news is flashed over
trembling wires to all the principal points, and the
press, with hungry avidity, seizes upon the minutest
incident of the tragic record for the edification of its
readers.   The departed one may not be endowed
with the double royalty of greatness and goodness,
for we all know that these qualities are separable.
It is sufficient that such a man has won the plaudits
of his fellow men, to be entitled to the esteem and
respect of his own race and the nation as well.

Master of Ceremonies: There was a period of
Grecian history denoted the heroic age.   The mystic
spirit of that classic race had invested men with the
dignity of gods. So wonderful had been their achievements, so exalted their career that the mere attributes

of ordinary humanity were not sufficient to account for virtues they possessed. Their names were inscribed upon the warrior's shield, lifted up as the silent guardians of the public weal and adorned the temple dedicated to justice.

In all places and on all occasions where patriotism sought an example, the heroes of classic Greece claimed the reverence and affection of the people.

We come here today as Mosaic Templars, gathered from the four corners of the United States to give higher witness to a human character, and to learn anew the lessons of value attaching themselves to the self-sacrificing spirit, the consecrated service and the immortal reward of that public benefactor, the lamented John E. Bush. It is right that we should pause in our avocations and while laying no garlands upon his tomb in yonder cemetery, we feel it befitting to give to the world the benefit of our sober thoughts as they relate to his value and service.

Society notes the vacancy when an educated and useful mind is withdrawn from its service. Society feels the loss of this great mind which in its period of youth, in its period of old age, in progress and decline, labored incessantly for the promotion of society's welfare. Like the oak whose withered branches have withstood the storms and gales of centuries, whose leaves have been strewn hither and thither by wailing winds, yet holds aloft its head amidst the angry blasts and rigors of winter, so did J. E. Bush gradually unfold himself from a small beginning, until as a result of his labor and toil, we have the Mosaic Templars of America—this helpful institution, born in the fertile brain of a Negro.

It was the dream and effort of the late J. E. Bush to leave this institution, without fault or wrinkle, so financially sound, that it would ever be an example to other Negro institutions.

Thirty-four years ago the inspiration came to Mr. Bush, with Keatts and others to establish this Order. It was instituted, not for the good of Mr. Bush, not for honor or glory, but for the betterment of his people.   Confronted with opposition, oftimes so powerful that it seemed to have been inspired from superhuman sources, he never once turned his face from the task before him.   Through floods and flames, assailed by foes and deceived by friends, he stood like Leonidas at the battle of Thermopylae.

After a struggle of thirty-three years, we now see his real greatness.   The plaudits of the nation bespeak the rugged route he traveled and the magnificent result of his enduring toil.   His labor will serve as an inspiration to unborn thousands, and wayfaring pilgrims, journeying from time to eternity will pause and look upon his work and press onward to the goal.

Yes, his life and work is inspiring to every intelligent and progressive son of Ham.   His accomplishments have been phenomenal.   Well has the poet, Longfellow, said:

> "Lives of great men all remind us,
>   We can make our lives sublime,
> and departing leave behind us
>   Footprints on the sand of time."

Another poet tells us:

> "Were I so tall to reach the pole,
>   Or grasp creation with a span;
> I'd still be measured by my soul;
>   The mind's the standard of the man."

When we look at the mechanism of man, we are astounded to note how wonderfully divinity displays its foresight in preparing for life's work. His limbs are devised for forward movement. The eyes are placed in front and above, forming the windows of a pilot house. These all being in front indicate that man's chief business is to be looking ahead and going ahead.

No man of our race used the faculties more than did our lamented J. E. Bush. Phillip Bailey has well said:

"We live in deeds, not years; in thought, not breaths; in feeling, not figures on a dial. We should count time by heart-throbs. He most lives who thinks most, feels the noblest, acts the best."

Of the many elements which go to make up the construction and stability of an organization, no elements is more delicate and yet more important than the financial element. Our race is blessed with many worthy gifts. But it is often said that when money is turned into our hands it mysteriously and suddenly disappears. Not so with our lamented and worthy J. E. Bush. How many times, yea, thousands of times, has his honesty been tested by the secretaries of various chambers, palaces and temples and was not found wanting.

In his work, in his life, in his very innermost being, J. E. Bush believed with Shakespeare:
"A good name, my Lord, in man and woman, is
the immediate jewel of their souls. He who steals
my purse steals trash. 'Twas mine; 'tis his, 'twas
something, 'tis nothing, and has been slave to thousands. But he who filches from me my good name,
robs me of that which enriches him not and makes me
poor indeed."

John E. Bush worked all his life to help others,
to promote worthy causes, to lend assistance in this
cause and that. For many years he was one of the
leading spirits in the National Negro Business Men's
League and was one of the few men upon whom
that sage and leader, the late Booker T. Washington,
depended upon to give tone and setting and influence
to this great organization. Next to Mr. Washington
himself, the father of the movement, John E. Bush
was one of its most important factors.

One can never forget his dictum: "It's no further
from New York to Little Rock than it is from Little
Rock to New York," that battling against the strong
sentiment that wished to keep the meetings of this
national body in the East and North, be by the force
of his own personality brought the meeting to busy
Little Rock, where for the first time the business men
of the nation were able to see for themselves what the
Negro men and women in the heart of the South
were doing. One need not dwell upon his work in
this great organization, the Mosaic Templars of
America, for you know full well what he has accomplished here, but he has made it possible for
Negroes to herd together their pennies and nickels

and dimes into one common treasury, for a particular purpose, go to sleep and wake up and still find that money there.

It is providential that whereas the confidence of the Negro people in the stability of Negro concerns and the ability of Negro men would be shaken every now and then by the honest failure of some or the mismanagement of others, that a man like Bush should be raised up and do for the Negro race that which seems so essential at this time—give them a worthy example of the combined strength of capability and honesty. One stalwart and strong and the other rigid and unshakable. I tell you, men and women, nothing looks better to me and to you than an honest man.

John Bush was the only Negro, in the heart of the South who got into office, remained there from year to year, from term to term, only to be displaced as the political exigency demanded on the assumption of power by the opposite party. John E. Bush was the only Negro holding Federal office in the heart of the South who could have done so as long as he lived and as long as his party remained in power. In the sixteen years he served this important station at Little Rock there was voiced no dissatisfaction, nor when his removal did come, was there any dissatisfaction voiced even by his political enemies.

If there are those who would laugh at the Negro's lack of preparedness for political office, we point to Bush. If there are those who say the Negro does not properly appreciate responsibility and the delicate sensitive points involved in the proper holding of a big political office, we fall back upon Mr. Bush's

record.   When the carping critics claims that the
Negro's cupidity and greed make him think more of
himself than of his people and makes the big and
successful Negro leave his people in sentiment, if not
in fact, we ask John E. Bush to give the lie to them.
He has done it by all these years of faithful, self-sacrificing labor for the black men and women of the
South.

"And Moses went up from the plain of Moab
unto the mountain of Nebo, to the top of Pisgah
that is over against Jericho; and the Lord showed
him all the land of Gilead, unto Dan."

Here we have a life ending in the midst of labor.
When from Pisgah's heights the promised land lay
outstretched before Moses, he must have felt that his
work was far from completion.   The tribes were
yet to be conducted over the rolling Jordan.   Jericho
with its massive defenses was to be taken, Hittites,
Perrizzites, Canaanites and Jebusites, all were to be
exterminated, the land divided among tribes, and
the theocracy fully organized.   But Moses must die.

Ah!   Thus it is ever with us.   Men for the most
part die in the midst of their labor.   It seldom hap-
pens that any in the last hour feel that they have
finished their work, that they have done all that they
might have done—proposed doing.

The farmer leaves his field half plowed.   The
artist dies with half-formed figures on the canvas.
The tradesman is cut down in the midst of his mer-
chandise.   The career of the statesman is arrested
with great political measures on his hand.   The minister departs with many schemes for instruction and
plans for spiritual usefulness undeveloped.

If other men die thus, we must infer that such was the case with our lamented J. E. Bush. He died in the midst of his labor. No one can yet tell or ever tell what great things he had in his mind for the good of the Mosaic Templars. It can be truly said of him, *Veni, vidi, vici.* "I came, I saw, I conquered." Can't we imagine Brother Bush looking into the future and seeing in advance the possible future greatness of this grand Order?

Mr. Bush's never-failing love to and for his family prepared them for the very lofty position of security so well fixed now. Let us see to it that they enjoy this.

What magnificent legacy he has turned over to his successors and the successors of others who were born into this world before the smoke of battle had cleared away. Now they bathe their souls in heavenly rest, yet they look down upon their successors and wonder how well their unfinished work will be carried on.

Moses looked down to Joshua. McKinley looked to Roosevelt; Booker T. Washington to Moton; Alexander to Elliott. So will J. E. Bush look to S. J. Elliott, C. E. Bush, L. L. Powell, John H. McConico, Scipio Jones and many others to keep the Mosaic Templars safe on the track of usefulness to mankind.

In the midst of his labor, died our friend and brother, John E. Bush, on December 11, 1916, at 11:00 p. m.

Servant of God, well done;
Rest from thy loved employ;
The battle fought, the victory won,
Enter thy Master's joy.

The voice at midnight came;
He started up to hear;
A mortal arrow pierced his frame;
He fell, but felt no fear.

The pains of death are past;
Labor and sorrow cease;
And life's long warfare closed at last,
His soul is found in peace.

Soldier of Christ, well done;
Praised be thy new employ;
And, while eternal ages run,
Rest in thy Savior's joy.

Mr. W. E. Dancer, Jacksonville, Florida, for many years the Grand Master of the Jurisdiction of Florida and at present filling very acceptably this position, contributed the following poem and read the same at the Memorial Exercises in honor of the departed leader.

Mr. Dancer is acknowledged the poet laureate of the Order and has written many verses dedicated to the Order, besides having published a volume of his poems which have been favorably received by a critical public.

JOHN E. BUSH

By W. E. Dancer, G. M. of Florida.

Oh! God our hearts within us ache,
  Our souls are filled with grief;
Now for Thy humble children's sake,
  Pray give us quick relief.

Reveal it in our conscience, Lord,
  Just why you take the best;
While we, with hearts not half so broad,
  Are left among the rest.

We had a lily in our field,
  A lily pure and white,
Wrapped in that great Fraternal Shield,
  He stood for truth and right.

Our J. E. Bush, the great Grand Scribe,
  The hero of our race;
The Mosaic's will hardly find
  A man to fill his place.

And Lord, it's not our race alone,
  But earth must feel this loss;
We know he's now around Thy throne,
  Lord, help us bear this cross.

WILLIAM EVEY DANCER
State Grand Master of Florida.

Born December 1, 1883, at Shorter, Ala.

Graduated in 1905 at Tuskegee Institute, Alabama.

Elected State Grand Master at the State Grand Lodge held at Jacksonville, Fla., February 18, 1918.

Approximate number of lodges in the State when elected, 5.

Approximate number of members when elected, 150.

Present number of lodges in the State, 125.

Present number of members in the State, 2,500.

Connected with the Order 14 years.

T. H. KING
State Grand Master of Mississippi.

Born January 15, 1893, at LaGrange, Tenn.

Appointed State Grand Master succeeding his father, who died in 1920, at Shaw, Miss.

Approximate number of lodges in the State when appointed, 102.

Approximate number of members in the State, 2,040.

Present number of lodges in the State, 135.

Present number of members in the State, 4,090.

Connected with the Order for 13 years.

LETTERS AND TELEGRAMS FROM SYMPA-
THETIC FRIENDS

As soon as it had been flashed over the wires
and announced through the Associated Press
that Mr. Bush was dead, telegrams and letters
came pouring in from every corner of the
country.   Space forbids publishing even a
very small portion of them.   We have selected
a few which are given here as typical of the
many.

Many of these letters were from white business organizations of his home city and are
proof of the high esteem in which he was
held by the men who knew him best.   These
tributes are from leaders and men of public
affairs of both races.

The daily press of Little Rock carried each
day mention in some manner of the deceased
from the time of his death until his burial.
The mayor of Little Rock made public ac-
knowledgment on behalf of the city of Little
Rock of the death of Mr. Bush, something
unusual in a Southern city the size and im-

portance of Little Rock. Every bank and business house of any importance sent letters of sympathy to the bereaved family, together with beautiful floral tokens. Nor should it be overlooked the small, but sincere floral tributes and spoken words of the hundreds of his friends of his own race in humble station who had learned to love the deceased and look upon him as friend and brother to whom they could come with their troubles and sorrows with the assurance of sympathetic audience and in many cases of financial assistance with the admonition not to mention same.

The following are representative tributes:

McRae, Georgia, December 12, 1916.
Dr. S. J. Elliott, N. G. M., Mosaic Templars of America, Little Rock, Arkansas.

MY DEAR DR. ELLIOTT—Your telegram disclosing the information that the Honorable J. E. Bush, N. G. S., M. T. of A., has fallen in sleep has just reached me at this place. I am profoundly shocked and grieved over the sad news. Beyond question a great man and positive benefactor of the race has gone to his well deserved reward. A reward the more deserving because his unceasing labors were directed toward the alleviation of suffering and provision against the needs of the future among the needy of his people.

May his great work, so nobly conceived and executed fall into none other than hands worthy to take up where he has laid down and thus make doubly secure to our people the achievements of a life dedicated to the highest and noblest purposes. Let the great Order he founded and loved so well live on to bless with ever-increasing benedictions the generations yet to be.

I very much regret that Annual Conference duties will prevent me from being at the funeral.

Fraternally yours,

R. S. WILLIAMS, *N. G. C.*

ISIAH T. MONTGOMERY
Land Agent for the Y. & M. V. Railroad
Dealer in Delta Lands
Mound Bayou, Miss., December 13, 1916.

Mrs. John E. Bush and Family, Little Rock, Ark.

VERY DEAR FRIENDS—We were inexpressibly pained to learn of the sad loss that has so recently befallen your household; and if it were possible to be away from home at this particular period, I should be personally present tomorrow to share more fully with the family and friends in their personal sorrow. From the earliest years of human existence it has been the lot of humanity to suffer unutterable pangs of grief over the ravages of the grim monster Death, notwithstanding the coming of our blessed Savior in human form to teach all who love Him that death is but the gateway to life more abundant, a more perfect entrance upon the heirship of our eternal omnipotent Father.

The temple of clay that loving hands shall so carefully put to rest is simply the earthly tabernacle of the noble individuality that so many of us joined with you in loving the real personality. The immortal soul has gone to a more perfect union and comprehension of the Divine Presence of the Great I Am, who gave it to bless and help you all and a host of loving friends.

The great and intrepid spirit may not come to us again in earthly presence, but it is ours to press on in the glorious faith that we shall overcome in the sweet bye and bye, and meet our loved ones again to be forever free from sorrow and pain.

We shall pray that the blessings of our loving Heavenly Father who tempers the wind to the shorn lamb, may abide in your household and give abundantly of that spiritual peace that passeth all human understanding and lights us to the end.

Sincerely yours,
ISIAH T. MONTGOMERY AND FAMILY.

THE MUTUAL LIFE INSURANCE COMPANY
OF NEW YORK
H. L. Remmel, Manager
Gazette Building

Little Rock, Arkansas, Dec. 15, 1916.

Mr. Chester E. Bush, Little Rock, Arkansas.

DEAR SIR—It was with regret that I read the account of the death of your distinguished father, because he was distinguished. Having risen from an humble position in life, he attained honors at the hands of his party in the Government, and he distinguished himself in founding a great order that will live to perpetuate his memory. He was a good citizen and he was a leader of his race, and his advice to his people was always in the right direction. He and Judge Gibbs will stand before them during the coming years as men that their race can point to with pride, and they are men that your children and the children of the colored race should try to emulate.

I regret that on account of the serious illness of my wife, I was unable to be present at the funeral.

Very truly yours,
H. L. REMMEL.

NOTE—Mr. Remmel is at present Republican National Committeeman for Arkansas, Internal Revenue Collector for Arkansas and Chairman of the State Central Committee of the Republican Party.

THE NATIONAL NEGRO BUSINESS LEAGUE

Tuskegee Institute, Ala., Dec. 15, 1916.

Mrs. J. E. Bush, Box 36, Little Rock, Arkansas.

MY DEAR MRS. BUSH—My beloved friend, and your good husband, has passed away. It hardly seems possible that we are not to see him again.

I sent you a telegram promptly upon receipt of the news from Mr. Scipio Jones that he had passed away, which was the first notice that I had received that he was seriously ill. I knew that he had been ailing for some time, but was unaware of the real gravity of his condition.

You, I am sure, have had from all of your friends expressions of deepest sympathy. That is all I can offer you, and yet I do wish you to know how sincerely Mrs. Scott and I, and all of your friends here who knew and esteemed him, regret his passing away at this time when we need his guidance more than ever.

Please remember us to the children who sorrow with you. I shall hope to be writing you again when my spirits will be less sad than they are now.

Sincerely and faithfully your friend,

GAS.   EMMETT J. SCOTT.

CITY OF LITTLE ROCK, ARKANSAS
EXECUTIVE DEPARTMENT
Charles E. Taylor, Mayor
Fletcher Chenault, Secretary

December 19, 1916.

Mr. Chester E. Bush, City.

DEAR SIR—On my return to the city I learned of the death of your father, John E. Bush. Please accept my sympathy and convey expressions of regret for me to the other members of his family. He was a man of great ability, much intelligence and resource, and as a leader did many practical things that will be remembered by both races in this city and state for many, many years. He was a good citizen and Little Rock will feel his loss.   Yours sincerely,

CET:R.   CHARLES E. TAYLOR, *Mayor.*

UNION TRUST COMPANY

December 15, 1916.

Mrs. J. E. Bush, Little Rock, Arkansas.

DEAR MADAM—I hope it will be a satisfaction for you and your children to know that the business men who knew your late husband have a high regard for his citizenship, and appreciation for the good work that he did among the people of his race.

There are very few colored men who have rendered so valuable a service to the community. We hope that some one will rise up to take his place, and continue the progressive work among his people. As you probably know, all the good white people have much pleasure and satisfaction in the successful development of the Negro citizens of Little Rock.

With much sympathy for your personal bereavement,

Yours very truly,

EAS:MW.   MOOREHEAD WRIGHT, *President.*

THE MUTUAL LIFE INSURANCE COMPANY OF NEW YORK

H. L. Remmel, Manager

Gazette Building

Little Rock, Ark., Dec. 14, 1916.

Chester E. Bush, Little Rock, Arkansas.

DEAR CHESTER—I was certainly shocked to hear of the death of your father. He was a great credit to the community, and has done more for his race than any other man in the State. His going will be a great loss to you all.   While he and I differed politically during the past few years, still I have always had a great respect for him, and I sincerely sympathize with you in your loss.

Very truly yours,

ACR:GC.   A. C. REMMEL.

IN MEMORIAM.

When I picked up the morning paper last Tuesday and read of the death of Hon. J. E. Bush, I was shocked almost beyond expression, notwithstanding the fact that I knew that he had been in failing health for several months.

My first expression after reading the report of his death was, ''No death which has occurred in this state has affected more people than the death of Mr. Bush.''

My acquaintance with Mr. Bush dates from August, 1881, when he was a young man of only 25 summers; that acquaintance soon grew into warm personal friendship, which was never broken, but grew warmer and stronger as the years rolled by.

When he and the late C. W. Keatts were planning to launch the Mosaic Templars of America, he cordially invited me to take part and become one of the founders but my ministerial duties prevented me from associating myself with them.

No one could foresee at that distinct day, the marvelous success which awaited the venture then being launched by those two young men; but it has grown to such wonderful proportions that it will not only be a blessing to humanity, but will ever be a crown of honor to the founders.

If Mr. Bush had done nothing more than give to the race the organization of which he had so long been the honored head, it would have been sufficient to give him a place in the affections of the people for all time to come.

But John E. Bush was more than the head and co-founder of the Mosaic Templars of America; he was a leader of his people in many notable respects as all the people of Pulaski County well know. For many years he had occupied the most prominent position as political leader of the Republican party in this county of any man in it. He was the logical successor to the late Judge M. W. Gibbs and was thus honored by all the people of the State.

His many years' service in the government land office, and as Receiver of public moneys, is the best evidence which can be given of his efficiency and integrity as a public servant. He was not always understood by his friends, but it can be said of John E. Bush that he was true to his race, and never put his personal interests above that of his race.

Mr. Bush had in him a philanthropic heart, which never turned down a worthy cause, but he was ever ready to help those he believed to be deserving, but above all the notable characteristics of that noble-hearted man, stood the fact that he was a Christian.

The teachings of a sainted mother, stood before him at all times, and he had no greater delight than to point to the fact that his mother was a devout member of a Baptist Church, and that he could not be anything other than what his mother was.

When we come to consider the beauties of the Christian life, all the notable achievements of our mortal existence fades from view; for that higher and better life connects us with the eternal joys on the other side of the river of death, and admits us into that existence which is indescribable, for it doth not yet appear what we shall be.

I am sure that it is very gratifying to the family and friends of Mr. Bush to know that while he lived a busy useful life on this side of the mystic river, he never failed to make his peace calling and election sure, and that nothing came up in this life to cause him to drop the cable of faith by which he has been drawn up from the bustling scenes of a transitory life to that city which has been prepared for all the faithful followers of the meek and lowly Jesus.

By E. C. MORRIS.

Helena, Arkansas, Dec. 14, 1916.

NOTE—The Rev. E. C. Morris, who wrote the above appreciation of Mr. Bush, was, up to the time of his death, President of the National Baptist Convention, which is the largest Negro organization in the world. No colored man who ever lived in America was better known than the late Dr. E. C. Morris and Arkansas takes pardonable pride in claiming him as one of her most distinguished sons.

The Arkansas Gazette gave the following account of the funeral of Mr. Bush:

(Arkansas Gazette, Dec. 15.)

Funeral services for John E. Bush, 60 years old, one of the wealthiest Negroes in the South, and founder of the Mosaic Templars of America, were held yesterday afternoon at the First Baptist Church, Seventh and Gaines Streets. Many Negroes, including high officers of the Mosaic Templars and visitors from all parts of the State attended. Several white persons also attended. The Negro schools were given a half holiday yesterday. Many floral designs, among them being one sent by the City of Little Rock, were received.

The exercises were in charge of P. H. Jordan, State Grand Master of the Mosaic Templars. Bishop J. M. Connor of the A. M. E. Church read Scripture passages, and the funeral address was delivered by J. H. McConico, National Grand Auditor of the Mosaic Templars. The Rev. J. P. Robinson, pastor of the First Baptist Church (Negro), also spoke. Roscoe Conkling Simmons, Negro orator and journalist, offered a resolution from the National Negro Business Men's League, which was founded by the late Booker T. Washington, and of which Mr. Bush was Vice President.

Telegrams of condolence were received by the Bush family from all parts of the South, among them being messages from the widow of Booker T. Washington, several officers of the Tuskegee Institute, officers of the Business Men's League and of the Mosaic Templars.

Bush was the organizer and Grand Secretary of the Mosaic Templars of America, which has more than 80,000 members in 26 States, South and Central America, the canal zone and the West Indies. He was receiver of the United States Land Office here for 16 years, and was a close friend of Booker T. Washington. He died at his home Monday afternoon, and is survived by his wife, a daughter and two sons. Last night the oldest, Chester E. Bush, was appointed to fill the position of his father as National Grand Secretary of the Mosaic Templars, and Aldridge E. Bush, the second son, succeeded his brother as Secretary and Treasurer of the Monument Department.

The remains of Mr. Bush lie in a beautiful mausoleum built out of Vermont Granite and was given as a memorial by the Mosaics throughout the National Jurisdiction. This mausoleum is erected on a commanding site in Fraternal Cemetery, the principal cemetery for the burial place of the colored of Little Rock and of which he was for many years one of the commissioners appointed by the city council.

WILLIAM ALEXANDER (Deceased)
NATIONAL GRAND MASTER

MR. WILLIAM ALEXANDER BECOMES
NATIONAL GRAND MASTER
A SHORT SKETCH OF HIS LIFE

At the time of the death of the Honorable
C. W. Keatts, Mr. Alexander was serving in
the position of National Aaronic Grand Master which was the equivalent of vice National
Grand Master. The law then provided for
the succession of the National Aaronic to the
Grand Master-ship in the event of a vacancy,
therefore at the death of the National Grand
Master, Mr. Alexander automatically became
the acting head of the order to fill the unexpired term of the deceased. So well did he
perform the duties, so suddenly thrust upon
him, that at the next national meeting held in
Paducah, Kentucky, in spite of strong con-
tenders for the place, he was elected to succeed
himself.

HIS BIRTHPLACE

Mr. Alexander was born in Columbus,
Mississippi, May 16, 1867, and spent the period of his youth at this place. He always

spoke with much pride of the fact that he had seen the light of day in Mississippi. As that State had produced a large number of eminent colored men, he undoubtedly was influenced by this fact, in his ambition to make of himself a useful man.

He had only the meager opportunities that were the lot of the average colored boy to secure an education from the limited course then offered in the public schools of his state. But as was characteristic of him, he got all out of the course which was offered. His later education was gotten from the school of experience in Arkansas, where he identified himself with such leaders as J. E. Bush, C. W. Keatts, Judge M. W. Gibbs, and many of the other leaders of the community. He was an apt pupil and soon attracted the attention of this group of experienced men who were ever in the alert to discover young men of exceptional ability.

By dent of hard work and exercising frugality, and by doing well all that his hands found to do, he acquired sufficient capital to

embark in business. For fifteen years he successfully managed a mercantile business, aside
from engaging in the work of a contracting
painter. He was a skilled artisan in that trade,
and through his reputation as an honest and
efficient contractor built up a large partonage.
He kept constantly employed twenty-five to
thirty skilled workmen, and only gave it up,
by reason of his duties as National Grand
Master.

Mr. Alexander became a Mosaic in 1905
and at once entered with heart and soul into
the work of the order, seeking in every way
its promotion and prosperity. His rise to
position and influence in this organization was
phenomenal. Being made National Aaronic
was no empty honor, for as mentioned before
this always carried with it the possibility of
succeeding to the head of the order. There
were some to speak of the luck of the man;
in this they were mistaken; what they called
luck was pluck, for had he not possessed the
qualities for such a possibility he would never
have been selected for the second place. The

National Grand Master was failing in health and there was ever present the possibility of the worst happening and another succeeding him. Therefore in naming a man for Aaronic Grand Master it would be the part of wisdom to select someone who would have the ability to fill the office of National Grand Master, in the event that this should ever become necessary. How wise they were in this selection will be instantly seen in a review of the work of Mr. Alexander as National Grand Master.

HIS ACTIVITY IN OFFICE

In filling out the unexpired term of his predecessor Mr. Alexander made no effort to initiate any new measures but was content to carry out the policies of his predecessor during the unexpired term. He set about at once in familiarizing himself with the duties of his new office and the detail of every duty devolving upon him and in the short time that intervened between the death of Mr. Keatts and the next national meeting which was held in Paducah, Kentucky, he had attracted the

most favorable attention. He impressed all
with the fact that the right man had been
elevated to this high position. He immediately won the esteem and affection of the rank
and file of the membership. He kept pace
with the most advanced ideas of fraternal
effort and at once began to lead the Mosaic
membership into the front rank of fraternal
work.

INAUGURATES THE PERIOD OF EXPANSION

After being elected National Grand Master,
having filled out the unexpired term of his
predecessor, he at once began to initiate new
ideas and a conquest for new members that
has never had a rival for results obtained.

In his first annual message to the National
Grand Lodge he recommended the erection of
a National Temple building whose site should
be in the city of Little Rock. The cost of this
Temple was estimated at fifty thousand
($50,000.00) dollars. This recommenda-
tion met the hearty approval of all of the associate officers and of the members. In a short

while thereafter the Temple was constructed,
but so rapidly had the Order grown that it
was found necessary to revise the original
plans and build a larger building somewhat
in excess of the original estimate of cost.
Oddly enough this building was erected on
the site on which an old frame shanty had
formerly stood and upon whose steps Mr.
Bush more than thirty years before would
sit and discuss with his little group of friends
his idea of founding an Order for the benefit
of the poor and distressed of the race. This
building is located on one of the most prominent corners of the business district occupied
largely by colored business, a source of inspiration not only to the Mosaics, but to every
member of the race. An idea of the numerical
strength of the organization at that time can
be gained when it is remembered that this
handsome and modern structure was erected
by levying a per capita annual tax of only
twenty cents per member and that the building was paid for before the estimated time.

S. E. TOWNSEND
State Grand Master of Missouri.

Born May 6, 1874, at Harvill, Butler County, Mo.

Elected State Grand Master at the Grand Lodge held in Poplar Bluff, Mo., August 19, 1919.

Approximate number of lodges in State when elected, 15.

Approximate number of members in State when elected, 300.

Present number of lodges in the State, 35.

Present number of members in the State, 1,200.

Connected with the Order for 5 years.

G. D. BRYSON
State Grand Master of Kansas.

Born December 27, 1872, at New Albany, Miss.

Elected State Grand Master at the Grand Lodge held at Kansas City, Kas., in 1917.

Approximate number of lodges in State when elected, 6.

Approximate number of members in State when elected, 650.

Present number of lodges, 25.

Present number of members, 2,500.

Connected with the Order for 12 years.

HE ADDS THE UNIFORM RANK DEPARTMENT

Another example of expansion and progress was creating the Uniform Rank Department. Mr. Alexander saw the necessity of the young men of the race having military training for its physical and disciplinary value and the only course open to them was through the fraternal orders, as every Southern State had debarred them from joining the State Guard. This department exceeded his most sanguine expectations and it was at once evident that it appealed to the young men of the race from the large number of applications received for membership.

HE LED A STRENUOUS LIFE AS NATIONAL GRAND MASTER

As National Grand Master, Mr. Alexander was never idle and had no patience with those who were. He was always on the alert for new fields of conquest for the Mosaic cause. He traveled constantly from State to State, always preaching the Mosaic gospel. His itinerary covered eighteen States and during the first year of his administration he added something like fifteen thousand members to the Order. Nothing like this had ever been done before, the entire organization was fired with zeal and enthusiasm. Alexander's name had become a word to conjure with; he had a method all his own, but a method which got results.

In this campaign, and throughout his administration, he had associated with him as his right bower a young man whom he had picked for this untried position. This was Mr. J. H. McConico. Mr. Alexander had a peculiar knack for picking the right man for the right place. He seemed to be possessed with an uncanny art in this direction; he would select raw and unheard-of material, often to the dismay of other officers of the organization, and when protest was made would only ask that he be given the opportunity to justify his selection, and seldom did he ever miss his guess in these selections. Mr. McConico, of whom more extended reference will be made in this work, was a young man of exceptional "horse sense" and with gifted eloquence. He and Mr. Alexander made a modern Paul and Silas combination, and with their fiery eloquence and untiring zeal, literally set the woods on fire with Mosaic enthusiasm, shooting conviction right into the hearts of all who would give them an audience and the Mosaics became the fastest grownig fraternal organization in the race.

Mr. Alexander was a man who had the courage of his convictions and by this sometimes found himself misunderstood. He adopted the motto of Davy Crockett: "Be sure you are right, then go ahead." He had no patience with drones or dishonest persons in the organization and was uncompromising in his attitude to them. Though he was a man of large heart and broad sympathies, when convinced that a man had acted dishonestly or dishonorably in office he dealt out quick and sure punishment.

The following extract from an address delivered by Mr. J. E. Bush at the National Grand Lodge meeting held in Tuskegee Institute, Alabama, sheds an interesting ray on the character of the man and his unyielding determination to break down every obstacle that stood in the way of what he deemed right and proper. Mr. Bush said:

When it dawned upon me that Mr. Keatts would not recover I was at sea as to what man to place his mantle around. I had been so much deceived and betrayed that I had little faith in mankind. I knew the great power and influence wielded by the head of the Order, and a man thus placed could easily destroy what I had been twenty-five years in building. In looking over the field my eye fell upon William Alexander. I had known him for years and a mental analysis showed me that he was a man who believed in making anything first class or nothing. That he was National Grand Master material I was hardly convinced. I had seen him take hold of church work and push it to success. I had seen him take hold of local lodges of the Odd Fellows, Pythians and Mosaics and raise them from wrecks and make well organized bodies of them. However, all of these were local examples. As a national executive he was an untried official at that time; men were scarce in the Order and of all those who aspired for office he loomed the largest. Hence, when Mr. Keatts passed away he succeeded to the throne.

No sooner had Mr. Alexander been inducted into office than he began to push and pull. His energy and enthusiasm seemed to have been without bounds. I have always been of an optimistic nature, but I

must confess that the energy and enthusiasm of Mr.
Alexander made me shudder. Many of his ideas and
opinions appeared to me as downright anarchy. The
result was his first year was barren of results, as the
time that should have been put in the field was spent
in trying to strike some happy medium between his
ideas of government and mine. At this time Alabama
was our most troublesome State. As fast as one thing
was settled something else crept up. We made Alabama his first trial. I was willing for him to go
there and do what he could do, but I will not confess
that it was a case of David placing the man in the
front of the battle line, because I had come to the
conclusion that I had made a mistake in selecting
him as the head of the Order. The first move that
he made he set aside all of the old appointees of Mr.
Keatts, and it looked to me that he placed in office
all of the fellows that Mr. Keatts had always kept
down. I looked for pandemonium to break loose.
He came in from Alabama and left the State at peace
and added more than three thousand members to the
Order on that trip, extending over six months. The
officials who had been removed confessed to a man
that he had shown them clearly that the work would
not grow under their administration, and they willingly gave away and fell in line. In that he demonstrated leadership of which I judged him incapable.
I began to regard him with more favor. The next
test was severe. There was an accumulation of claims
in the office aggregating about four thousand dollars.
They were rank frauds on their face, cases where
members had died non-financial, but by collusion
with their local lodge officials they were financial in

their subordinate lodge. Every lodge official knows just what you are up against when you go to court with this kind of claim. The whole lodge will combine against the Grand Lodge, and you will lose every case thus contested. These claims were turned over to Mr. Alexander and when he returned he brought the Grand Lodge a clear receipt for all of the claims that had been settled for one thousand five hundred dollars, which was less than it would have cost us to resist them in the courts. Here he demonstrated that he was an executive. Naturally, I thought that wherever he had settled one of these claims that the Order had been destroyed. The records show that, on the other hand, he had added members to all of the lodges, and in many places had organized new lodges. Again, I noticed that in spite of my opposition, preventing many of his plans from being carried out, he never sulked in his tent, but worked right along and never tried to retaliate. His earnestness and sincerity stood out in his every move. A man whose motives are pure can be relied upon. We now understood each other and joined hands for general uplift. Today we can boast of being king of the field. Our record stands out in bold relief.

HIS ASSASSINATION AND DEATH

Grand Master Alexander died a martyr to the principles of the Order and to devotion to duty.

As has been observed in this story Mr. Alexander was uncompromising with wrong-doers of the Order. He felt as head of the Order it was his sacred duty and solemn obligation to guard well every interest of the Order. His policy was to "Hew to the line, let the chips fall where they will or may." M. H. Harrison, who had been honored in various capacities by the officials of the Order had been appointed State Grand Master for the Jurisdiction of Kentucky. He and Mr. Alexander had been friends for years, and although Harrison's conduct in office had not been all that an upright official's should have been, Mr. Alexander with his usual magnanimity of spirit, tried to save him over the protest of the counsel of his friends. Harrison's conduct went from bad to worse and finally in sheer desperation it was necessary for the National Grand Master to remove him from office and have him report to headquarters at Little Rock. He came, his case was thoroughly gone over; he assumed a penitent attitude and once more Mr. Alexander gave him an opportunity to make good. During the interval of being out of office Mr. Alexander personally cared for the material needs of Harrison and he, Harrison, pledged his unswerving loyalty to Alexander and the Order. With differences apparently adjusted Mr. Alexander, together with his trusted friend and adviser, J. H. McConico, accompanied Harrison to Kentucky where he was reinstated and given a deputyship. Everything seemed in perfect harmony. Harrison apparently was well satisfied with the provisions made for him.

On the morning of November 1, 1913, while Mr. Alexander and Mr. McConico were seated in the office of Dr. Underwood, a prominent physician of Frankfort, Kentucky, Harrison rushed into the office, and without a word of warning, fired on Alexander with a double-barreled shotgun, causing instant death.   Apparently it was his purpose to also kill McConico, but McConico grappled with him and succeeded in disarming him.

Harrison was arrested and indicted for murder in the first degree.   The prosecution was assisted by the legal representative of the Order, Judge Scipio A. Jones.   The accused entered a plea of guilty as charged in the indictment and is now serving a life term in the penitentiary at Frankfort.

The remains of the lamented Alexander were met at the station in Little Rock by a sorrowing multitude of Mosaics and personal friends.   His funeral was held from the First Baptist Church of which he had for many years been a member.   Little Rock was grief-stricken over the tragic taking away of one of her most distinguished citizens.   The funeral was one of the most impressive ever seen in the city.   His remains were laid to rest in the Fraternal Cemetery.   A beautiful monument erected by the National Department, fittingly inscribed, marks his resting place.

Immediately after his death his widow, Mrs. Minnie Thomas Alexander, to whom he was married in 1889, was granted a pension for life by the National Department, in recognition of the splendid services her lamented husband had rendered to the Order. At the National Grand Lodge meeting in Tuskegee, Alabama, memorial services were held in memory of Mr. Alexander. More than two thousand people were present.

The Rt. Rev. R. S. Williams, Bishop in the C. M. E. Church, delivering the principal eulogy assisted by Bishop G. W. Clinton of the A. M. E. Zion Church and the Rev. J. W. Goodgame of the Baptist Church.

J. FRANKLIN WILSON
*State Grand Master of District
of Columbia.*

Born June 28, 1886, at Talladega, Ala.

Joined the Order upon its admission to the District of Columbia, was appointed Grand Master. A fraternal man of wide experience and holds exalted positions in other fraternities.

Present membership of jurisdiction, over 500.

J. N. DRUMMOND
*State Grand Master Canal Zone,
C. A.*

Born in Jamaica, British West Indies, January 28, 1880.

Educated in school of Parish Westmoreland.

Served on constabulary force, with rank of corporal.

Left for Canal Zone and was sent to the States as Special Envoy to learn about the Mosaics. Returning to the Canal Zone his report was so favorable that application for charter was made in 1913 and was appointed Grand Master in 1916.

There are now nine subordinate lodges, with nearly 500 members.

Chapter II

THE BIRTH OF THE MOSAIC TEMPLARS OF AMERICA AND ITS EARLY HISTORY
1882 TO 1895

During recent years there has been a deal of varying speculations and reasons advanced as to why, when and where the Mosaic Templars of America was organized. It has been published in the form of advertising matter, the exact reasons; and so stated in a very excellent address delivered by Mr. J. E. Bush, the National Grand Scribe of the organization, at the National Grand Lodge held at Tuskegee Institute, Alabama, in July, 1914. Excerpts from his speech are as follows:

The old adage that "He who works for humanity works for himself," is fittingly demonstrated in my labors for this Order. Most men who institute movements generally have some selfish motive, either for glory or profit. I could not truthfully tell you that I have gained either in my work of building up the Mosaic Templars. However, I will say that thirty-two years ago, when C. W. Keatts and I founded the Mosaic Templars of America, I had no ambition

leading toward glory nor any desire to make money
out of the enterprise.   Thirty-two years ago there
was no precedent for such.   All of the orders of that
day were run purely for benevolent purposes and the
day of high-salaried officers was unheard of, therefore, there was nothing to give birth to such an idea.
What was true of the financial end was true of the
other.   No men at that time had grown great as the
head of any fraternity.   In fact, they were little
known or considered.   On the other hand, both Keatts
and I were among the few Negroes that were in the
railway mail service.   We were drawing $100.00 per
month salary, and it may seem strange to you, but
a salary of $100.00 per month was then a bigger
thing than $500.00 per month now; hence, you can
see that I had no need to make any sacrifices for financial gain, as Keatts and I were commonly called well-
to-do Negroes.   I was ambitious to be prominent
as a leader, but I had tasted the sweets of political
contest and had mapped out for myself a political
career.   Thus, as I stated in the outset, financial
gain or glory did not enter the equation when the
grand work of the Mosaic Templars was laid.

The one thing above all others that inspired me,
as well as Mr. Keatts, to attempt the organization of
an Order of this nature was an effort to put a stop
to the public solicitation of funds to aid sick people
or bury the dead.   It used to be a common thing to
see some one with a list soliciting funds to bury some
poor person whose family was unable to defray
funeral expenses.   I have so often been embarrassed
while talking to some prominent white person when
some old colored woman would come up and ask for

a donation to bury some colored man who had been a citizen of the community all his life and had held good positions. The white man would often give her the donation and then turn to me with an oath and ask, "Why Negroes did not save some money in order that they could be buried decently when they died." Here the thought was given birth which finally culminated in the organization of the Mosaic Templars of America. The idea was a success and we were soon rewarded to the extent that the habit of soliciting funds with which to bury the dead gradually passed away. After the general public was made aware that anyone, by paying a few cents a month, could be given a decent burial, public aid was refused.

The continual listening to such comments and slurs, as those, by members of the other race, put Mr. Bush to much shame and he immediately set about with his associate, Mr. Keatts, to try to remedy this dishonorable condition among his people in Little Rock.

As he states further:

The evil which we started out to remedy was a local one, and our idea was to found a small benevolent or mutual association for the sole benefit of the people of this community.

As the purpose was only to correct local conditions, plans were laid and with a little band of thirteen persons the first lodge was organized known as Zephro Temple No. 1, on May 21, 1882, at Little Rock, Arkansas, which now operates and has upon its roll the only surviving member, Brother J. A. Davis, P. N. G. M.

The organization of this lodge formed the nucleus around which has been built the now magnificent institution. The formation of this branch, however, does not mark the beginning of the business career of the institution, because one year lapsed before the Articles of Incorporation were filed and the charter granted to do business, which was May 24, 1883. The date of filing of the Articles of Incorporation was on May 22, 1883. And we can therefore feel safe in saying that the Mosaic Templars of America began business as a fraternal society on that date.

The operations of the Order existed for some years before the opportunities that afforded it to do a greater business dawned upon its founders, and further Mr. Bush says:

The benefits to Little Rock were self-evident and the city was singing the Order's praise. The thought came to be that similar conditions existed in other cities and the people needed relief. I asked myself the question: Why the Order could not be established in other communities?

It was therefore, at this point that Bush and Keatts had the vision of the now mighty institution. Due conference was held between them and the small band of followers and all thought exceedingly well of the idea of expansion, but none took a willing hand in lending financial aid, excepting the two men who fostered the idea. It was discovered that in accordance with the few existing laws that then governed them, they could not easily expand their operations unless separate branches were organized for both men and women. The Temples for men and Chambers for women. Consequently, out of Zephro Temple No. 1 grew Lone Star Chamber No. 1, which is now in operation and has upon its roll a few of the surviving members. The original charter of Lone Star Chamber No. 1, which is now in the sacred archives of the

Order, shows that this lodge was not permitted to function as a local branch until August 6, 1883, but was formally instituted on August 2d of the same year. The original charter of Zephro Temple No. 1, which is also carefully preserved, shows that it was chartered June 25, 1883, and instituted August 1, 1883. The operations of Zephro Temple No. 1 proper were hindered on account of the inability, at that time, to get a sufficient number of men interested; consequently, this lodge did not really become chartered and authorized to do business until as late as August 1, 1883, however, its formation dates as far back as May 21, 1882.

The original charters of these parent local branches show the following persons as having made formal application for charter rights:

Lone Star Chamber No. 1—Sisters M. E. Pryor, Mollie Ballard, Annie Johnson, Bettie Campbell, Jennie Ballard, *et al.* Of course, there were others who participated in the setting up of this branch but their names do not show; only enough names appearing to conform to the law.

Zephro Temple No. 1 shows as chartered members—Brothers R. May, J. A. Davis, G. R. M. Reeves, S. M. Ballard, S. W. Williams, O. T. Berry, J. C. Campbell, R. B. Robertson, B. Kagel, C. C. Jeffries, R. N. Mangrom, J. T. Thomas, *et al.* The same explanation as given in the account of the Chamber is given for the nonappearance of certain names on this charter. The putting into operation of these bodies was the real beginning of the business career of the Mosaic Templars of America.

An exact copy of the original charter, as was granted, is herein given. These exact words are taken from literature dating as far back as 1888, only a few years after its birth. This particular piece of literature is entitled "Constitution, General Laws and Proceedings of the Grand Temple, held at Hot Springs, Arkansas, September 11, 12, 13 and 14, 1888," and can be accepted as authentic. The charter reads as follows:

CHARTER

Be it known that J. E. Bush, C. W. Keatts and W. L. Arrington, and others are hereby constituted a body politic and corporate by the name and style of "Mosaic Templars of America," under the laws of the State of Arkansas, which reads as follows: "An Act to incorporate benevolent, industrial, co-operative and other associations, for the promotion of good and useful purposes," approved February 23, 1875.

The general objects of said corporation are as follows:

1. To unite fraternally all persons of good moral character, of every profession, business and occupation.

2. To give all possible moral and material aid in its power to members of Mosaic Templars by holding instructive and scientific lectures; by encouraging each other in business and assisting each other to obtain employment, but shall not interfere with religious or political opinions of any of its members.

3. To establish and maintain a benefit fund from which any sum not to exce d two thousand dollars ($2,000.00) shall be paid t he member, to his family, or as he or she may direct, t expiration or his or her life policy, or at death.

4. The general power of said corporation shall be to sue and be sued by the corporate name; to have and use a common seal, which it may change at pleasure; or if it has no seal, the signature of the name of the corporation by any duly authorized officer will be legal and binding; to purchase and hold, or receive

by gift, ᴄ uest or devise, in addition to the personal property owned by the corporation, real estate necessary for the transaction of the corporate business; and also to purchase and accept any real estate in part payment to any debt due the corporation, or to sell the same; to establish by-laws, and to make all rules and regulations, not inconsistent with the laws of the land, devised expedient for the management of corporate affairs; to charter subordinate Temples; to make its own constitution, laws, discipline and general laws for the government of the entire Order in America; to fix the compensation of its officers, and to do whatever may be necessary for the government of the grand and subordinate Temples, not in conflict with the laws of the United States or the State of Arkansas, and not in conflict with the objects and powers of this charter.

Witness our hands this 24th day of May, 1883.

J. E. BUSH,

C. W. KEATTS.

We, the undersigned officers of the Mosaic Templars of America, herewith request the granting of the above charter, and ask for a certificate as by law required.

C. W. KEATTS, G. M. W.

J. E. BUSH, G. S.

JOHN H. JOHNSON, G. I.

CERTIFICATE

Office Circuit Clerk, Pulaski County, Ark.

Little Rock, May 24, 1883.

Whereas, C. W. Keatts, John E. Bush, W. L. Arrington and others, have filed in the office of the clerk

of the Circuit Court of Pulaski County, their Constitution or Articles of Association, in compliance with
the provisions of the law with their petition for incorporation, under the name and style of "Mosaic
Templars of America." They are therefore hereby
declared a body politic and corporate, by the name
and style aforesaid, with all the powers, privileges
and immunities granted in law thereunto appertain-
ing.
                          Attest: J. L. BAY,
    (Seal)   Clerk of the Circuit Court of the said
                    Pulaski County, and Ex-Officio Recorder.

In this "Proceedings of the Grand Temple
held at Hot Springs, Arkansas, September,
1888," is also contained a copy of the original Constitution, upon which the present day
organization has been firmly built.

CONSTITUTION
Article I
NAME AND POWER

1. This organization shall be known as The
Grand Temple of Mosaic Templars of America, with
power to make its own Constitution, Laws, Rules
and General Laws for the government of the entire
Order.

2. It shall be the body to which all appeals shall
be made on all matters of importance emanating from
Templars or any source, working under the authority
of the Grand Temple of Mosaic Templars.

Article II
OBJECTS OF THE ORDER

1.   The object of the Mosaic Templars shall be to unite fraternally all good, healthy and acceptable persons of good moral character of every profession, business and occupation.

2.   To give all possible and material aid in its power to members of the Order.

3.   To establish a benefit fund, from which a sum not to exceed two thousand ($2,000.00) dollars shall be paid at the expiration of the life policy or death of each member in good standing, to his family, or as he or she may direct.   One assessment settles in full whatever amount collected.

4.   To establish a fund for the relief of sick and distressed members.

Article III
POLICIES AND HOW PAID

The policies of the Order shall be divided into two classes, to wit: At the expiration of policies, which is at the age of 65 years, or if initiated between the ages of 60 and 65 years, you must at least be a member of the Order for six years; or at the death of any member of this Order, who was sound in body and mind at his or her initiation, and was not subject to any complaint that caused them to be a burden to the Grand Temple or their Temple or Chamber, and during membership paid all their dues in their Temple or Chamber, also the Grand Temple, upon satisfactory proof of all such expirations or deaths the Grand Temple shall pay each claimant an equal proportion of the annual death tax of one dollar collected from each member, but in no case shall such sums exceed two thousand dollars, one payment ordered by the Grand Temple next ensuing shall settle in full, whatever be the amount.

Article IV

POLICIES AND HOW DIVIDED

1. The policies of the Order shall be divided into three classes, to wit:

Class A, age from 15 to 35 years.

Class B, age from 35 to 55 years.

Class C, age from 55 to 65 years.

Payable in the following order, at death or expiration:

Class A, 15 to 20 yrs., expires in 40 years, $2,000.00
Class A, 20 to 25 yrs., expires in 35 years, $1,700.00
Class A, 25 to 30 yrs., expires in 30 years, $1,500.00
Class A, 30 to 35 yrs., expires in 25 years, $1,250.00
Class B, 35 to 40 yrs., expires in 20 years, $1,000.00
Class B, 40 to 45 yrs., expires in 15 years, $ 750.00
Class B, 45 to 50 yrs., expires in 10 years, $ 500.00
Class C, 50 to 55 yrs., expires in 9 years, $ 450.00
Class C, 55 to 60 yrs., expires in 8 years, $ 400.00
Class C, 60 to 65 yrs., expires in 7 years, $ 300.00

The taxation for matured policies shall be 10 cents each; for death, 25 cents for each policy; the annual tax shall be 25 cents.

2. At death or maturity of any policy, members shall pay according to the class to which they belong, but shall not receive any amount to exceed $2,000.00 as per capita, to which class they belong.

3. All moneys collected per capita from classes A and B to pay policies in Class C, that exceed his

per capita, and the same in Class A to pay Class B, shall create a sinking fund to be used as the Grand Temple may direct.

4. Upon satisfactory proof of the death of any member in good standing, or maturity of his or her policy, the same shall be paid in sixty days after proof (in case of maturity), but in case of death, thirty days.

Article V

1. The officers of this Order shall be: One Grand Mosaic Master, one Grand Aaronic Master, Grand Scribe, Grand Treasurer, Grand Chaplain, Chief Grand Deputy and his associates, Grand Warden, Grand Inside Guardian, Grand Outside Guardian and Grand Marshal; all of whom shall serve for the period of one year, or until their successors are elected and qualified; provided, however, that the Grand Mosaic Master and Grand Scribe shall serve until all policies taken under them shall have matured and been paid. All other officers must be commissioned by the Grand Mosaic Master.

2. The G. C. of M. shall be composed of the Grand Mosaic Master, Grand Aaronic Master, Grand Chief, Grand Treasurer, Grand Scribe and four members elected by the Grand Temple, which shall constitute the Grand Head of this organization, and shall transact the general business thereof.

3. The C. of M. shall meet quarterly or oftener, if necessary, beginning the first Tuesday in January, April, July and October, and five of the members duly assembled shall constitute a quorum, and shall have full power to conduct the business of the Order

according to the laws for the government thereof;
and shall, in all things, act for and in the name of the
Order, and all orders and acts under the power dele-
gated to them shall have the like force and effect as
the acts and orders of the organization at any meeting of the Supreme Grand Temple.   Every question
at such meeting shall be decided by a majority vote.
The Grand Mosaic Master shall have the casting vote.
The Grand Mosaic Master must convene all extra
meetings of the committee.

4.   The Grand Mosaic Master and Grand Scribe
shall meet on the second Tuesday in each month to
grant dispensations, etc., and to perform such other
business as may properly come before them; provided
that the business transacted by them shall be reported
at next quarterly meeting of the G. C. of M.

GRAND MOSAIC MASTER

5.   The Grand Mosaic Master shall preside at
meetings of the Com. of M. and the Grand Temple,
and enforce all the laws thereof.   He shall have
the general superintendence of the Order.   He shall
institute the quarterly password, and, with the assistance of the Grand Aaronic Master and Grand
Scribe, the same shall be furnished to all Temples
in good standing.   He shall sign all orders on the
Grand Treasurer drawn according to law.   He shall
sign all documents and papers that require his signature to properly authenticate them.   He shall fill all
vacancies caused by death or otherwise.   He shall
have power to revoke the commission of any officer
of this Temple or Order.   He shall have power to
establish Temples and make passes in degrees.   He

shall have power to appoint and commission any Brother as a Deputy Grand Mosaic Master to superintend in establishing Temples, or to perform any other business pertaining to the good of the Order. He shall have power to suspend any Temple working under the charter of the Mosaic Temple, when failing to comply with the Constitution and Grand Laws of the Order. He shall either visit or deputize some authorized officer to visit each subordinate Temple once each year before the meeting of the Grand Temple. He shall make out a full and complete statement of the condition, etc., of each subordinate Temple, together with his actions, and report the same to the Grand Temple. He shall receive such salary and give bond in such sum as the Grand Temple may deem just and proper.

GRAND AARONIC MASTER

6. The Grand Aaronic Master shall preside in the absence of the Grand Mosaic Master, and in case of death, resignation, disqualification, refusal or neglect of the Grand Mosaic Master to discharge the duties of his office shall then perform all the duties incumbent upon the Grand Mosaic Master until an election shall be held. He shall have the power to establish Temples and visit the same when inconvenient for the Grand Mosaic Master to do so. He shall advise with the Grand Mosaic Master, and keep him cognizant of his movements.

GRAND SCRIBE

7. The Grand Scribe shall keep a correct report of the proceedings of the Grand Temple and C. of M. He shall read all reports, communications, petitions, etc.,

and attest all orders drawn on the Grand Treasurer.
He shall affix the seal to all documents when necessary.
He shall prepare the annual and other reports for
publication, and shall make a report to the C. of M.
once every quarter, unless otherwise ordered by the C.
of M. He shall, at each annual meeting of the Grand
Temple, make a complete report of the condition
of the Order. He shall, immediately after the proof
of death of a member in good standing, or maturity
of valid policy held by member entitled to benefits,
draw an order on the Grand Treasurer for the amount
due, and forward same to the scribe of the subordinate
Temple of which the deceased was a member, or
policy held. He shall also cause the same to be published. He shall, after drawing such order, ascertain
the amount that will be left in the treasury, and if
less than two thousand ($2,000.00) dollars, to im-
mediately forward the scribe of each Temple a notice
of assessment. He shall with the advice and consent
of the Grand Mosaic Master, furnish for publication
in the quarterly circular such items of interest as may
come to his knowledge. He shall conduct the correspondence of the Grand Temple and C. of M., but
nothing shall be considered binding without the signature of the Grand Mosaic Master. He shall keep
a record of the name, number and date of initiation,
and location of all the Temples, also name, age and
occupation and residence of each member of the Order.
He shall have charge of the seal, books and papers
belonging to the Grand Temple, and shall keep a
true and correct account between the Grand Temple
and the subordinate Temples, and at each annual
session of the Grand Temple shall make a full and

correct statement of all moneys received and disbursed during the year. He shall receive all moneys due the Grand Temple, and shall, at the end of each month, make a settlement with the Grand Treasurer, and pay over all moneys belonging to the Order. He shall make a financial and numerical statement each quarter to be published in the quarterly circular, and shall perform such other duties as the law and usages of the Order may require. Before entering upon the discharge of his duties he shall give bond in such sum as may be required by the Grand Temple or C. of M., and for his service shall receive such salary as may be deemed proper and just.

GRAND TREASURER

8. He shall hold and keep secure all moneys received by him, and, with the assistance of the Grand Mosaic Master and Grand Scribe, shall deposit the same in some substantial bank, and shall not keep in his possession more than twenty-five dollars ($25.00) at any one time, unless ready to be paid out. He shall pay all orders drawn on him in accordance to the law. He shall keep a correct account of all moneys received and paid out by him. He shall keep his books regularly posted and ready for exhibition when required by the C. of M. He shall make to the C. of M. a full report of the condition of the treasury every quarter. He shall make a corrrect and full report to the Grand Temple at its annual session yearly. At the end of his term or when called on shall turn over all books, papers, moneys, and such other property as may belong to the Order. He shall, before entering upon the duties of his office,

give bond in such sum as the Grand Temple or C. of M. may require, for the faithful performance thereof, which bond may be increased from time to time, as the Grand Temple or C. of M. may deem fit. For his services, he may receive such salary as the C. of M. may deem proper and just.

CHIEF GRAND DEPUTY

9. The Chief Grand Deputy shall examine the books of the Grand Treasurer and Grand Scribe at the annual meeting. He shall examine reports of all subordinate Temples when sent to the Grand Temple. He shall make a full and complete report of all proceedings of the Grand Temple. He shall perform the duties of the Grand Mosaic Master in the absence of the Grand Mosaic and Aaronic Masters. He shall have power to establish and visit subordinate Temples when commissioned so to do by the Grand Mosaic Master. When visiting any Temple, if fraud and corruption are found to exist, he shall immediately suspend the same and report his action to the Grand Mosaic Master for his approval or rejection. He shall associate his deputies with him in making reports, etc. He shall receive such pay as the Grand C. of M. may deem just and proper.

OTHER OFFICERS

10. The Grand Chaplain, Grand Marshal, Grand Warden and Grand Inside and Outside Guardians shall perform all duties required of them at their several stations in the Order.

Article VI
LADY CHAMBERS AND PALACES

1.   The Lady Chambers and Palaces of this Order shall be governed by the Constitution, laws, etc., as other Temples, and shall be under the special watch-care and guardianship of the Grand Mosaic Master.

Article VII

1.   This Constitution shall be and is in force from the date of approval by the Grand Mosaic Master.

2.   The Grand Temple shall not pass any ordinance, resolution, law or part of the law that will conflict with this Constitution, but shall remain as the supreme law of this Order.

Approved by C. W. Keatts, G. M., September 9, 1886.

The above Constitution has only been amended in a few instances.   Such amendments that have been made were for the purpose of conforming to surrounding conditions and to meet the requirements of the various insurance laws of the several States in which we operate.   Of course, in the early days of the Order's existence no such rigid insurance laws, as are now, were then operative.

SITTING OF FIRST GRAND LODGE AND
ITS EARLY PROGRESS

So eager were the pioneers of this organization to place the Order before the public, in
the way of a demonstration, the first Grand
Lodge was called to meet in the city of Little
Rock, Arkansas, in September, 1883, at
Schader's Hall.   This Grand Lodge was only
attended by fifteen or twenty delegates, but
the usual business was transacted and, it is
said by a few of the surviving ones, that a befitting demonstration was had, which proved
to be the needed attraction to gain members.
So, from the sitting of this Grand Lodge it
can be said that the Mosaic Templars of
America began to grow.

The organization met with its trials and
tribulations as all new ideas do.   The principles and motives were severely ridiculed and
slandered and it appeared that as soon as they
looked forward to development, they would
be forced to drop back in a rut that seemed
almost impossible to overcome or master.   But
it was plainly demonstrated that the more op-

positon the harder they worked to conquer.
Most of their setbacks, strange to say, were
the result of treachery and disloyalty among
their own workers.   Those kind of workers
with a determination to "rule or ruin." They
did, however, conquer over such enemies and
succeeded in placing the Order on a very firm
foundation.   This opposition did not last
long, but was rather the cause from which
has grown an organization of strength and
solidarity.   Other Grand Lodges were held
at Little Rock, Ark., 1886; Hot Springs,
Ark., in 1888; Augusta, Ark., 1890, and
Lake Village, Ark., 1892. During this lapse
of years, it is shown by its history that the
Order was gradually gaining because at the
Hot Springs, Ark., meeting the Credential
Committee, composed of M. F. Cox, chairman, Mary Burnette, Addie Maurice, and H.
Ferguson, rendered a report of 103 delegates
as being registered.   At this same meeting the
report of the Grand Scribe showed receipts for
the year 1887, from all sources, of $1,345.20.
Of course, this does not in any way approach

the present day yearly collection, but it is a good showing taking into consideration the various obstacles and hindrances with which they had to come in contact.

It has been said by some, that the Order was at one time abandoned and was forced to undergo re-organization. But from all authentic sources, such as records, chartered members and older citizens of Little Rock, it has been reliably established that the organization has never ceased to function since the date of its beginning.

ORIGIN OF ITS NAME

It has often been a question in the minds of many, whether or not the success of the organization does not partly, if not wholly, depend upon the reason that the entire secret works were designed after the life of Moses, who was one of the most outstanding figures in biblical history. To those who are familiar with the organization, they agree that it is built and operated entirely upon all the principles of Christianity. The oppressed conditions of the Negro at the time of organization

H. P. STEWART
State Grand Master of Kentucky.

Born November 24, 1876, at Belmont, Ala.

Appointed State Grand Master of Florida in June, 1915, and served 3 years.

Appointed State Grand Master of Kentucky by S. J. Elliott December 9, 1921.

Approximate number of lodges when elected, 82.

Approximate number of members when elected, 1,250.

Present number of lodges in the State, 162.

Present number of members in the State, 4,284.

Connected with the Order for 13 years.

J. W. REDDICK
State Grand Master of Tennessee.

Born September 2, 1880, at Franklin, Tenn.

Elected State Grand Master at the Grand Lodge held at Jackson, Tenn., August 30, 1922.

Approximate number of lodges in the State when elected, 220.

Approximate number of members in the State when elected, 5,000.

Present number of lodges in the State, 251.

Present number of members in the State, 7,000.

Connected with the Order since 1917.

were in such deep resemblance to the conditions of the Children of Israel that, in designing the Mosaic Templars of America, the founders were moved to make the selection of the life of Moses as the basis for the principles around which to build the Order. So, it is readily seen that the Mosaic Templars were designed from the very beginning as an organization of love and charity and also as a medium of giving protection and leadership to members of its race as did Moses to the Children of Israel. Hence, the founders, in making such a selection, had no alternative other than selecting a name for the Order that would reflect the story around which the secret works were written. So, the first name given was that of "The Order of Moses," under which they operated until a formal application for a charter to the State of Arkansas was made. A few days prior to making application, the little band met and upon suggestion the name was changed to that of "Mosaic Templars of America," in which name the charter was granted in 1883, under

which the organization yet operates. In relating these facts, we are reminded also of the
sound business management that has accompanied it and which has played a good part in
its growth.

THE MOSAIC NATIONAL BUILDING AND LOAN
ASSOCIATION

The Mosaic National Building & Loan
Association was organized in 1884 by Messrs.
J. E. Bush, C. W. Keatts and S. G. Garrett
as an adjunct for the Mosaic Templars of
America. It was organized exclusively for
the benefit of the members of the Order and
for the purpose of aiding them in the purchas-
ing of homes, relief from pressing mortgages,
and to give financial aid in general. This
Association was only formed with the inten-
tion of operating for a limited time. That
is to say, until the Order proper was well
enough hedged in with financial resources to
assure the membership of the protection that
was promised. This was an act of wisdom
and precaution.

The Association was duly recognized and authorized at the Grand Lodge meeting held at Pine Bluff, Ark., in September, 1884, after which the Articles of Incorporation were drawn and the charter applied for and granted. It was managed by a competent set of by-laws and compared favorably with any of the present building and loan associations. The original literature, bearing upon this association, points out the fact that it was operated in "chain" form with the home office at Little Rock, Arkansas and was a stock concern.

The officials were as follows:

C. W. Keatts, President.
J. E. Bush, Secretary.
Solomon Winfrey, Vice-President.
D. G. Hill, Assistant Secretary.
John Jeeter, Treasurer.

Directors—C. W. Keatts, Solomon Winfrey, John Jeeter, D. Mitchell, J. H. Stephens, A. B. Moore, J. E. Bush, C. E. Smith, S. G. Garrett, D. G. Hill, W. L. Cook.

It operated and functioned successfully until 1895, at which time the Mosaic Templars of America had grown to such an extent that it was financially able to care for its members, and by common consent of all parties concerned the association was dissolved. All stockholders being paid in full for every dollar invested.

The following is a copy of the Articles of Incorporation taken from an old copy of a pass book then used for the purpose of receipting the various members of the association:

ARTICLES OF INCORPORATION

Know All Men by These Presents:

That we, the undersigned, by virtue of and pursuant to the provisions of an Act of the Legislature of the State of Arkansas, entitled "An Act to Provide for the Creation and Regulation of Incorporated Companies," approved April 12, 1869, have associated and do hereby associate ourselves together for the purpose of being incorporated under said act, and according to the provisions thereof, as a joint stock company, to carry on business as hereinafter designated, and do hereby agree upon the following Articles of Incorporation.

Article I

The name of said corporation shall be the Mosaic National Building and Loan Association, Perpetual.

Article II.

The place of business is to be located at Little Rock, and other places in the United States, and its principal office for the transaction of business shall be in Little Rock, Arkansas, or at such other place as the board of directors may select.

Article III

The general nature of the business proposed to be transacted by the corporation is to accumulate funds by subscription to its capital stock and to advance said funds, or portions thereof, to its stockholders who may desire same, upon such terms and conditions as the by-laws may prescribe, and for such other investments as said corporation may deem proper and may sanction in its by-laws, and to furnish to stockholders who may not desire to borrow from the association an easy and profitable method of saving and investing their money.

Article IV

The amount of capital stock of said corporation will be two million five hundred thousand dollars ($2,500,000.00), to be divided into one hundred thousand (100,000) shares of twenty-five ($25.00) dollars each, to be issued in series numbered, respectively, I, II, III, IV, V, VI, etc., in the order of their first issue; each series to embrace not exceeding twenty thousand (20,000) shares of five hundred thousand dollars ($500,000.00) of stock in each; the first series to be numbered I, and new series to be issued from time to time as the board of directors may direct. Said association may commence business when fifty thousand dollars ($50,000.00) of said stock shall have been subscribed for.

Article V

The affairs and business of the corporation shall be conducted and controlled by the board of directors, consisting of nine (9) members, all of whom shall be stockholders of the corporation. Said board of directors shall elect one of its members as president, one of its members as vice-president, and shall also elect secretary and treasurer.

Article VI

The board of directors are empowered to ordain and establish all by-laws and regulations necessary to the management and business of said corporation, and alter or repeal same at pleasure.

From the dissolution of the Mosaic National Building and Loan Association, or from the year 1895, the organization proper seemed to take on its second permanent growth. The influx of members since that date has been marvelous. At that time there were more than 2,500 members upon the roll of the books of the secretary and an annual income of about $3,000.00. Although its field of operations did not comprise but a few States, it had seventy-seven chartered lodges composed of Temples, Chambers and Palaces. Its basis of operation, however, was confined mostly to Arkansas and Alabama, but the records show that some scattering business, not of consequence, was done in Mississippi, Texas and Tennessee. This scattering business was only attempted for the benefit of those members who had made their future homes and places of location in these distant States, but through this scattering business much of the expansion of the organization had its beginning.

Chapter III

Growth and Expansion

As was stated in the previous chapter the Order began its second growth at the close of 1895 and in the following States it began active business, but some of the early dates of entry as are shown, do not signify that the usual rigid legal test was put upon the organization before it could transact business, because it has only been until recent years that the various State insurance department laws have become so strict. However, the Mosaic Templars' growth, financial strength and competent management have at all times given justice to its being allowed to transact the business of a fraternal society and has at all times met every State requirement or test that has been placed upon it.

Of course, its first beginning of business was in the State of Arkansas on May 21, 1882, but it was, however, not chartered until May 24, 1883. The balance of the States and foreign places of operation are listed in chronological order:

Alabama _____June 15, 1887
Georgia_____September 10, 1901
Missouri_____July 27, 1902
Texas_____February 28, 1903
Louisiana_____July 17, 1903
Oklahoma_____November 12, 1904
Mississippi_____August 30, 1906
Tennessee_____August 30, 1906
Kentucky _____March 26, 1908
Florida _____March 16, 1911
Central America_____December 26, 1911
Virginia_____May 31, 1912
Kansas_____May 12, 1915
West Virginia_____March 1, 1917
Delaware _____April 18, 1917
New Jersey_____April 27, 1917
Maryland_____May 12, 1917
Illinois _____October 11, 1918
Pennsylvania_____June 16, 1920
Ohio _____September 14, 1920
Arizona _____December 19, 1920
Michigan _____March 31, 1921

Nebraska _____May 25, 1921
North Carolina _____June 1, 1922
District of Columbia_____December 21, 1922

A phenomenal growth has been enjoyed in
the above States and countries and none have
encountered any serious setbacks on account
of any deficiency of the organization.   Difficulties, however, have been met with, due only
to the economic conditions of the times but
considering such, a state of constant prosperity has accompanied the Order.

Much of the Order's history is naturally
built around Arkansas and has been recited in
the foregoing paragraphs.   A deal, however,
has been lost but enough regained to relate the
true and fundamental facts of interest; and
quite a sufficient amount to narrate, in
chronological form, its beginning and yearly
growth.

ADMISSION TO STATE'S RIGHTS

The business of the organization was about
this time getting so voluminous in every respect that after due counsel by the leaders,

and by popular sentiment of the membership, State's Rights were deemed necessary. Of course, in the declaration of these rights the centralized powers of the Endowment Department were not disturbed in the least but remained intact. In fact, the operations of the National Department were not at all impaired, but to a very great degree were strengthened. Prior to this time the entire management of affairs was in the hands of the national officials.

Through his farsightedness and the desire for the organization's growth and expansion, Brother P. H. Jordan, the present State Grand Master of the Jurisdiction of Arkansas, began the very unpopular movement for the adoption of State's Rights at the National Grand Lodge meeting of 1903 held at Poplar Bluff, Mo. Of course, he did not expect to have the sentiment fully crystallized at this meeting; he did, however, gain enough attention and support to lay the plans before the body. At the National Grand Lodge of 1904, held at Jackson, Tennessee, he continued his fight,

and at this meeting the idea had gained proportions to the extent that an almost decisive
vote was cast in favor. The two unsuccessful
attempts did not at all dampen his efforts, but
to the contrary developed in him a stronger
determination to effect its passage. So, at the
sitting of the National Grand Lodge, July 18-
22, 1905, at Memphis, Tenn., State's Rights
were finally declared, upon resolution submitted by Brother P. H. Jordan.

The result of this battle put him in much
disfavor with the powers, because from its
very beginning Brother C. W. Keatts, National Grand Master, disapproved of it and
only through the persistent efforts of Brother
Jordan, the continual persuasion of Brother
Keatts' friends and the convincing arguments
put to him that no ultimate weakness could
come to the Endowment Department (which
is the foundation of the Order) as the result
of its passage, that he finally decided to give it
his support. Through the declaration of
State's Rights a new growth in the Order was
quickly shown and the development has been

J. LEO MOORE
State Grand Master of Virginia.

Born March 14, 1873, in Polk County, North Carolina.

Elected State Grand Master at the Grand Lodge held May 16, 1923, at Petersburg, Va.

Approximate number of lodges in State when elected, 12.

Approximate number of members in State when elected, 190.

Present number of lodges in the State, 48.

Present number of members in the State, 1,000.

Connected with the Order for 17 months.

R. E. POPE
State Grand Master of Ohio.

Born July 31, 1888, at Hutchings, Ga.

Elected State Grand Master at the Grand Lodge held at Dayton, Ohio, September 27, 1923.

Approximate number of lodges in the State when elected, 56.

Approximate number of members in the State when elected, 2,000.

Present number of lodges in the State, 70.

Present number of members in the State, 3,500.

Connected with the Order for 8 years.

amazing since that time and placed it upon, a firmer foundation.

Prior to this period no special history is attached to the growth of the individual State jurisdictions; no more so than would embody the history and natural consequence of happenings. At this meeting, the various State officials, for the several States in which the Order operated, were appointed by the National Grand Master, C. W. Keatts, for a term of one year; and every year thereafter regular elections for these official places have been held in the State jurisdictions in conformity to the resolution creating same, which reads as follows:

Whereas, we believe it for the better working of the Mosaic Templars of America, and that its Temples, Chambers and Palaces and membership will be greatly increased;

Therefore Bt It Resolved, That this National Grand Temple at its twenty-third sitting in the city of Memphis, Tenn., July 18-22, 1905, do hereby agree and grant unto the several States of the United States, State's Rights to all States having seven (7) Temples or Chambers working in financial condition.

And It Is Further Resolved, That all States that may institute Grand Temples under this resolution shall be governed by the following Constitution and Laws:

Section 1.   All charters for the organization of Temples, Chambers and Palaces working under the jurisdiction of the Mosaic Templars of America shall be obtained from the National Grand Temple and prices paid therefor as stipulated in the Constitution and Laws of the National Grand Temple.

Sec. 2.   All policies held by members of the Order shall be bought from and obtained of the National Grand Temple, as now set forth in the Constitution and General Laws of the Mosaic Templars of America, as now provided or may hereafter be provided by the National Grand Temple.

Sec. 3.   The regulation for payment by members to keep said policies alive shall be made by the National Grand Temple.

Sec. 4.   All seals and paraphernalia worn by the members of the Order, or regalia of whatsoever kind, shall be obtained and bought from the National Grand Scribe-Treasurer of the Mosaic Templars of America.

The following States, at this time, comprised the Mosaic jurisdiction: Arkansas, Alabama, Missouri, Texas, Louisiana, Oklahoma, Mississippi, and Tennessee, with barely a total membership of 5,000 and assets not in excess of $15,000.00.

ADDITION OF BURIAL AND MONUMENT
DEPARTMENTS
BURIAL DEPARTMENT

The several State Burial Departments are peculiar in their origin, in that no national law has ever been passed authorizing them, but to the contrary, there exists no law that forbids its operation. However, the authority to make the needed annual assessments, perfect the various systems needed in its operations, was granted by the National Committee of Management upon recommendation of the late National Grand Master, Alexander, after a thorough test was given the operation of such a department by the jurisdiction of Texas in 1911. A later law was nationally adopted, as is shown by the General Laws.

Of course, the membership of this particular jurisdiction was called upon for a final vote after the lapse of the year's test and it was overwhelmingly passed. This jurisdiction so successfully managed this work and the idea was taken to so readily by the Texas membership that the National Committee of

Management unhesitatingly endorsed it and permitted those States to adopt it that saw fit. Consequently, the Arkansas jurisdiction followed the pace set by Texas and authorized its creation by popular vote in the State Grand Lodge of 1912 held in the city of Helena. During this same year, and the year following, the other jurisdictions adopted it with very slight difficulty.

These departments have proved beneficial to the membership by providing an adequate sum as a benefit for the burial expenses of the deceased members. In so doing, it has greatly relieved families, widows and orphans of possible embarrassments and been the cause by which those members of humble circumstances could be decently buried.

The system of management of these departments is solely under the guidance of the various State jurisdictions as to the amount of assessment levied and amount of benefits given. Hence, the assessments and benefits given are not uniform—ranging from one dollar to two dollars per member as assessments and benefits of thirty dollars to seventy-five dollars. The numerical strength of the jurisdiction governing this point.

In some of the jurisdictions these departments are so well managed that large cash assets have been accumulated. Most notably, are the jurisdictions of Louisiana and Alabama. Only in a few States are these departments not profitable. In no instance, however, has any of these departments been unable to pay its claims because of lack of support or refusal of temporary aid from some of the stronger departments of the Order.

At this point, it can be emphasized that this organization was the first among fraternals to offer such benefit and all new States entered are now required, before being recognized as a full-fledged State Grand Lodge, to organize such a department and give an adequate benefit.

MONUMENT DEPARTMENT

The idea of both the Burial and Monument Department was conceived simultaneously, but that of the Monument Department was taken with more favor by both the officials and membership. As a result, at the National Grand Lodge meeting held at Little Rock, Ark., in July, 1911, a law was enacted authorizing the creation of this department. It was not to be operated solely as a State feature, but in those States whose membership would justify it were granted such rights. The weaker jurisdictions were forced to operate from a central office. This office was supported partly by a full contribution from some States and a 10 per cent contribution from those States which operated independently.

This method of operation continued until the National Grand Lodge held at Tuskegee Institute, Ala., in July, 1914, when upon recommendation of S. J. Elliott, N. G. M., it was discontinued. This form of management was entirely too burdensome and awkward and the overhead expense connected gave good cause for the change.

The idea of the department was not abandoned, but the entire national jurisdiction was placed under a centralized head and the various State offices consolidated. Through this revision this department grew into the second strongest branch of the Order.

The featuring of this form of benefit is also first claimed by this organization.

The operations of this department as national in scope were formally begun September 1, 1915, and a review of its growth since that time is given in following pages.

ITS MANAGEMENT

The management, or government of this institution is modeled after that of the United States Government. It has three distinct divisions in its management, viz: Executive, Judicial and Legislative. These divisions and their various subdivisions are officered by a very efficient group of men and women, some of whom are considered experts in their particular line of work, and the office system employed compares favorably with any other concern of its size.

The system of collection of the dues and taxes is on a quarterly and annual basis and carried on by the secretaries of the local branches, who are properly bonded. Practically no overhead expense is attached to this system, other than the maintenance of an adequate accounting and general office force. The expense of operation is reasonably low and the Order has not yet been forced to levy any extra assessment to defray the general expenses. The National Annual Tax (the annual contribution paid by each member to defray the running expenses) remains the same as it was when the Order began business.

The three main divisions of the Order are divided as follows:

1. *Executive.*
   (a) General Supervision.
   (b) Accounting.
   (c) Auditing.
   (d) Health.
   (e) Extension.
   (f) Publicty.
   (g) Juvenile.
   (h) Military.

2. *Judicial.*
   (a) Litigation.
   (b) Rendering of Opinions.

3. *Legislative.*
   (a) Law-making.
   (b) Selection of officers (National Grand Lodge).

Added to the efficiency of these main divisions is the constant employment of a competent and well trained actuary, who supervises generally the office work of the Order, prepares rates and sees to it that the proper reserve fund is maintained. This phase of the work is not a legal requirement, but a duty that the officials deemed wise to adhere to for the protection of the policy-holders. Consequently the Order has never been embarrassed because of its inability to meet its financial obligations.

Chapter IV

ITS ACHIEVEMENTS

NATIONAL PROPERTIES

The success of the Order is not only reflected in its great accession of a membership of 108,000, but it stands out singularly from other fraternals of the race in the accumulation of large reserves in real properties. Its national headquarters located in the city of Little Rock represents a total outlay of $200,-000.00, having upon these premises two elegantly appointed and modernly equipped office buildings. The annex building, a two-story structure, serves only for the purpose of housing the various national departments of the organization. The main building, a four-story edifice, contains rented office suites, store-rooms and a spacious auditorium.

The national hospital site, located in the city of Hot Springs, Ark., is also a part of the national properties. This site contains seven acres of the city's most choice property and has a market value of $60,000.00. Upon this site, it is hoped to erect a modernly equipped hospital and sanitarium for the care of the sick and disabled members of the Order. A more descriptive idea of the wonder of this proposed building is given elsewhere in this volume.

STATE PROPERTIES

The erection of the National Temple was only the beginning of the plan to erect such buildings in each State jurisdiction. Since the inception of the idea, the States of Arkansas, Alabama and Louisiana have purchased sites and erected buildings that are creditable to any institution. The States of Texas, Tennessee and Oklahoma have also purchased sites and plan the early erection of suitable buildings.

These various "temples" are used for the housing of the State officials, as well as producing a revenue to each respective jurisdiction. In order to finance the building operations of these structures, a per capita tax was assessed and in this way no outside aid has ever been solicited. The combined cost of the real estate and buildings belonging to these various jurisdictions represent an investment of $280,000.00, which is included in the total assets of the Order.

A REVIEW AND DESCRIPTION OF DEPARTMENTS

ENDOWMENT DEPARTMENT

The Endowment Department is the bedrock upon which the Mosaic Templars of America was built. The entire plan of the mighty structure is encircled by this one department. With it alone, the organization will exist and continue to grow. Without it, the Order would fade into oblivion. So, in the very founding of the Order, most necessarily this department was created. The early history, as has been narrated, and as regards the growth and expansion, was naturally related to this department and nothing can be said of the Order without including it.

GENERAL OFFICE—ENDOWMENT DEPARTMENT

The department has been fortunate in its management, both in regard to the individual heads of this particular department and the Order in general. In its incipiency, this department had nothing in dollars and cents, as the organization is purely a fraternal concern and was not designed for profit or gain. With a membership of a few, from its meager beginning it has enjoyed a steady growth and has now an enviable cash balance, and other assets, as well as a multitude of members.

This department is under the direction of the National Grand Scribe and Treasurer, whose actions and conduct in office are subject to the supervision of the governing bodies, namely, National Grand Temple, National Committee of Management and National Executive Committee. This department is also subject to the very rigid examinations and scrutinies of the various State insurance departments. Into this department comes the funds from the Endowment, Juvenile, Monument, Temple, Uniform Rank, Mosaic Guide, Medical and Adequate Rate departments. It can readily be seen that the Order's entire volume of business is done through this department.

In the beginning, the first officer selected for this responsible position was Mr. J. E. Bush, who held said office until his death December 11, 1916, covering a continuous period of thirty-four years. During his term of office the department's growth was parallel with that of the Order's and at his death there were 38,604 members and with assets of $181,455.36. These assets did not cover the entire wealth of the Order in 1916, because the other departments of the several States, and of National Department also, were not included. The number of members as shown, however, are actual.

After the death of Mr. Bush, the duties of this office were placed upon his elder son, C. E. Bush, who by virtue of his long training in some of the less important positions of trust, in the Order, was selected without a dissenting voice. He served in this capacity, actively, until, through a very sad affliction

which came to him by his diligent application
to his duties, and was forced to give up work,
temporarily, November 19, 1921. The membership at this time according to the annual
statement which is submitted to the insurance
departments, showed a total of 75,315 and
assets of $665,904.53. Quite a stupendous
growth in both membership and assets for a
period of thirty-nine years. A. E. Bush, the
younger son, was selected to carry on the work
of this department during the incapacity of
his brother.

This department at the end of the year
1922 shows an actual membership of 87,069
and assets of $677,406.18. During its forty
years of existence no serious setbacks have
been encountered, and it has at all times tri-
umphantly weathered the storms of financial
depression and other slumps. Even through
the trying times of the 1918 influenza epi-
demic all claims were promptly paid without
the slightest embarrassment. Its history will
show that the contributions to this department have steadily increased, but at all times

the officials have kept in mind the safety of the organization, because any failure in this department would result in a fatal loss to the Order.

The annual income alone for the endowment purposes total over $475,000.00 and pays annual death losses of $250,000.00. This vast amount of money is paid largely to widows and orphans. This department affords employment to more than twenty young men and women and is operated on a flat quarterly premium of $1.25 per member for which a benefit of $300.00 is given. During the 1923 membership campaign 20,000 members were added and were accepted only under the strictest medical examination. The operations of this department comprise the whole of the National Jurisdiction. (States and countries are mentioned in preceding pages.)

MONUMENT DEPARTMENT

The National Monument Department was created at the Eleventh Triennial Session held at Tuskegee Institute, Alabama, July 21-25,

1914, through recommendations contained in the annual address of the National Grand Master, S. J. Elliott. This department had been operated by the several States as State departments, and was so organized; but through the business foresight of Mr. Elliott, seeing that the overhead expense connected with operating this department under several heads, created an enormous operating expense, his recommendation was adopted and the department placed under one central head or government.

It naturally consumed a deal of time to check out and close the various State Monument Departments and it was not until September 1, 1915, that the central office was absolutely established and placed into running condition. As the operation by the several States was not profitable to the Order, no cash surplus of any size had accumulated in any of the treasuries, however, the balance with which the central office was started has enabled the department to run without extra assessment being necessary. It now has a yearly collection of $45,000.00, and furnishes a monument to each deceased member of the organization. This monument compares most favorably with any given by any Order and is a great credit, and has proven a most valuable form of advertisment. The department is now considered indispensable in that it has been the means by which so many of the graves of the deceased members would have been lost to the world had it not been for these monuments being furnished.

At this point it can also be said that the Mosaic Templars boasts of being the first Negro organization to introduce the system of giving monuments to deceased members and included as part of the benefits derived.

Upon the centralization of this department, Hon. D. G. Hill, a man who had followed the organization since it early days, was selected as its secretary-treasurer. He served creditably in this capacity until his death. He served also in other important posts of the Order. Upon his death Mr. J. E. Henderson, another who had also given much of his attention to the Order, was selected as successor and who served until the need of the service of a matured mind to edit the Mosaic Guide was so pressing that he was called upon to resign in order to accept the office of editor. He filled this position with credit to himself and the organization. Upon his resignation, C. E. Bush, the present National Grand Scribe and Treasurer, was called upon to serve as his successor in this office. His tenure in office was marked with a great degree of business ability and satisfaction to the membership. His elevation to the position which he now occupies was the only cause for his resignation December 16, 1916. A. E. Bush was then appointed by the National Grand Master and this position is now being filled by him in connection with his duties in the Endowment Department, which department merged with the Monument Department July 1, 1922. This merger has proven most acceptable to the membership and in fact has reduced the operating expense of this department to a minimum, yet giving the desired amount of service. This department had, at the time of its merger, eight well trained clerks in its employ and is the second largest financial department of the Order. It is financed by an annual tax levy of fifty (50c) cents per member for which each deceased member receives a well-designed, uniform Vermont marble marker, with suitable inscription.

NATIONAL TEMPLE DEPARTMENT

The business farsightedness and shrewdness of the late Wm. Alexander, N. G. M., cannot in any way be questioned. It is found, in reveiwing the growth of the Order during his tenure in office, that each idea and plan that was advocated by him materialized to the mutual good of all. In his annual address to the National Grand Lodge held in the city of Paducah, Kentucky, July 20-25, 1908, he recommended that the creation of this department be done; either by resolution or amendment, and to be known as the National Temple Department. This idea was thought well of from the very beginning and

HEADQUARTERS

met with practically no opposition. Consequently, the law creating this department was enacted at this meeting. Up to this time no other Negro organization had especially provided for itself a headquarters and domiciled in such an imposing structure as was authorized and erected. The Mosaic Templars of America were the first to make this venture.

The first collection of this assessment was made in the following year and each subsequent year thereafter. Each member of the jurisdiction rallied well to this call, but of course, the first few years of collection did not in any way net enough to carry the proposition through to conclusion, but a loan from the Endowment Department of $45,-000.00 enabled the Temple Board to successfully finish the job.

The building housed the various offices of the Order adequately until 1918, when the volume of business became so great that more spacious quarters were absolutely necessary. In view of this fact, an annex was built. The total cost of these two buildings and grounds

represents an outlay of $200,000.00, includ-
ing furniture and fixtures, etc.

A period of fourteen years was covered in
the operations of this department; which
comprised the receiving and disbursing of the
funds of this proposition. The work was effi-
ciently done under the directions of the National Grand Scribe and Treasurer, J. E.
Bush, Brother C. S. Johnson of Arkansas
City, Ark., and Brother A. W. Weatherford
of Texarkana, Texas, as the only two treas-
urers. The latter having been first selected
and served until 1911, when Brother Johnson succeeded him.

At the National Grand Lodge held in Little
Rock, Ark., July 19-22, 1921, the membership was relieved from any further payment
of this Temple assessment after June, 1922,
and the department was abolished, having
served its purpose.

The maintenance of these buildings is now
derived through income from rents, and the
erection of them only manifests the progressive spirit which was and is in plain evidence

among the officers and members of the organization and simply proves what can be done by united effort. It was an outstanding achievement and shall stand for years to come as a monument to those who fostered and supported the idea.

JUVENILE DEPARTMENT

The Juvenile or Palace Department is as old as the Endowment Department, having its beginning with the birth of the organization. It has not operated at all times, independently of the other departments of the Order. In the beginning and up to 1911 it operated as a part of the Endowment Department proper. Its local branches met and transacted their business with Chambers, or female branches, under the name of "Lady Chambers and Palaces." This is true, as you will observe from the original Constitution under Article VI, Section 1, entitled "Lady Chambers and Palaces."

Up to the present time the workings of the local branches of the Juvenile Department are yet under the watch-care and guidance of some

female member of the Order whose official
title is "Worthy Guardian."

This department was severed from the Endowment Department because it was thought,
and wisely so, that a more speedy growth
could be effected by it operating to a certain
extent under its own management. Then
too, complaint came from some of the State
insurance departments, in whose States the
Order operated, objecting most seriously to
carrying this department as a part of the Endowment. And naturally the organization
was, if it intended to continue operations, to
abide by the State laws. Hence, the separation.

It has always been considered by the officials and insurance experts as the most solid
of the various departments. From the very
nature of this department, it has not enjoyed
at any time so large a cash surplus as the Endowment Department, but taking into consideration the risks that are covered by insur-
ing those of ages up to sixteen years, it can
readily be seen that the liability attached is

to a very great degree lessened. The death rate in this department has never exceeded its expectations and it has at all times maintained a very good growth. In recent years its growth has been exceedingly fine.

The agitation for the severance of this department from the Endowment was brought on by the late National Grand Master, Wm. Alexander, soon after his induction into office in 1908.

His fight was carried successfully to the National Grand Lodge, held in the city of Little Rock, Arkansas, July, 1911, when in his annual address he made recommendation to the body to place this department to itself and his recommendations were accepted, enacted into law with a small number dissenting.

After the adoption of this law, Mrs. C. C. Bell was elected National Grand Guardian. She has served in this capacity ever since and served with much honor. Under her, the department has grown from a membership of 680 to 4,582, and from assets of $52.00 to

$26,851.06. Its membership is comprised of boys and girls from the States in which the organization proper operates with but a few exceptions.

This department is maintained by a quarterly contribution of twenty-five cents and for which a benefit is given of fifty dollars. It also is permitted to participate in the benefits of the Burial Departments in the States in which it operates. It has not, however, ever been admitted to the benefits of the Monument Department.

The growth of this department has mainly been attained since 1911 and under the leadership of its present head, Mrs. Bell, who directs the field forces only. The funds derived from this department are handled through the office of the National Grand Scribe and Treasurer. In recent months much stress and attention have been directed to this department, as the officials have awakened to the absolute need of its development. During the big 1923 membership campaign, over 2,000 members were added to this department alone. More steady and constant growth has never before been enjoyed by this department of the organization.

MEDICAL DEPARTMENT

In the formation of the Medical Department the health of the membership was mainly borne in mind by those who contemplated the idea and perfected the plan; and this was the paramount reason that prompted its creation. Although in latter years the State insurance departments made it a necessary requirement for all secret societies for the protection against bad risks thereby making their business less hazardous. Hence, it is seen the importance that must necessarily be attached to this department.

The authorization of this department was made at the National Grand Lodge held at Paducah, Kentucky, July, 1908, upon resolution submitted by Dr. J. G. Thornton, who is at present the National Grand Medical Examiner. Of course, as in all new projects, some opposition sprang forth. This opposition, on the part of a near-sighted few, was

quickly subdued and the resolution was made
into law.

This department has successfully functioned to the great benefit of the Order since
its creation. It has proven to be indispensa-
ble, in that through its doorway must come
each applicant and there passed upon as to
physical fitness. It is extremely valuable in
giving scientific lectures upon health and hygiene; thereby, teaching the membership the
principles of proper and healthful living.
These are the main duties of this department.

By the persistent efforts of the head of this
department to absolutely safeguard the health
of the membership, at the National Grand
Lodge in 1917 held in Little Rock, Ark., a
law was passed authorizing the erection of a
general hospital and sanatarium. Of course,
the "hospital idea" is very popular with the
colored fraternals and coupled with the very
encouraging and successful work of past years
carried on by this department, the membership quickly saw the good that could be derived from such a project and with an almost

PROPOSED NATIONAL HOSPITAL AND SANITARIUM, HOT SPRINGS NATIONAL PARK

unanimous vote favorably passed the law authorizing its erection.

This proposed building, however, has not been erected, but preliminary sketches have been drawn (as shown on accompanying pages) and a most beautiful site has been purchased in the world-wide known health resort, Hot Springs National Park, Arkansas. The site is composed of seven acres in the heart of the city and is easily accessible to the health-giving waters of this resort. The location is most fortunate, being on a very high eminence, on a busy boulevard and only a short distance from the Missouri Pacific and Rock Island stations.

A general idea of the proposed building has been presented to the Executive Committee and is pictured as an imposing five-story structure of brick and steel built in H shape with a very spacious public lobby and reception room at the entrance. The left wing of the first floor is to be devoted entirely to offices, examination rooms, laboratory and x-ray departments and the right wing of this floor will be given over entirely to hotel accommodations. The whole of the second and third floors will be given over to the hospital patients. The fourth floor containing the dining and serving rooms with easy entrance to a roof garden, which will prove highly beneficial for semi-invalid and convalescent patients. On the fifth floor is to be found the kitchen and its accessories. The entire basement will be devoted to hydrotherapy, baths, storage, etc. The capacity of this building will be approximately two hundred and fifty beds for patients and about twenty-five for guests. Equipment of the very latest design and all accessories will be installed with the one thought in mind of affording sanitation, comfort and rest for the patients.

If this plan is materialized, it will be this department's most crowning effort as the use of the hospital facilities by the membership will be general and by so doing the death rate would be greatly reduced. The idea has met with encouraging endorsements thus far from the public, as well as the membership at large.

MOSAIC GUIDE

It is indisputable that no business can be successfully operated unless it indulges in a certain amount of advertising in one way or another. Seeing the necessity of this, the founding of the Mosaic Guide as the official mouthpiece of the Order was done soon after the perfection of plans to operate the Order were made. The exact date of the launching of this paper is unknown, but it can be safely said as early as 1885, judging from records, etc., this near date is authentic.

This paper had its origin from the paper then owned and controlled by Mr. J. E. Bush, known as the "American Guide," said paper being turned over absolutely for the use of the organization as its official organ under the present name "Mosaic Guide," with Mr. Bush serving as editor and manager. After this was done the operation of the paper was somewhat handicapped and about the latter part of 1886 its publication was discontinued. But through demand from the membership, it was ordered revived at the National Grand

Lodge meeting held in the city of Hot Springs, Arkansas, during September, 1888, by the enactment of a law providing for such. The committee on new laws proposing said law was composed of J. A. N. Phillips, chairman, Mary M. Burnette, C. M. McIntosh, Thomas Daniels, Mattie Thomas, and J. N. Andrews. This law was adopted by an overwhelming vote. Since that date the paper has been in continuous operation. It has not been operated with a profit and was never designed to be, yet it has been self-sustaining.

As the Order grew the paper grew also, because of its support coming entirely from a compulsory subscription fee from the various local branches. The duties of editor grew too burdensome and as a result Mr. Bush was compelled to resign as such officer in order to devote his attentions to the office of the Endowment Department. He resigned in favor of D. G. Hill, who edited and managed it successfully. Mr. Hill was succeeded by C. E. Bush, who also can share in the favorable results obtained. During the latter part of 1915

J. E. Henderson was made editor and served until July, 1921, at which time the management was placed entirely in the hands of National Grand Master Elliott, who chose as successor to Mr. Henderson Dr. D. B. Gaines, who now occupies this office.

This department developed wonderfully and until 1922 it had its own plant sufficient to turn out each weekly issue in a first-class workman-like manner, but upon orders of the National Committee of Management, this plant was disposed of, although the paper is still being printed and prepared for press in this same plant and at a very low cost to the organization.

Much favorable comment is received relative to the composition and class of news matter contained in this journal. It is only operated for the sole purpose of the Order and devotes its entire columns to such news.

UNIFORM RANK DEPARTMENT

The Uniform Rank Department was added to the Order through a law enacted at the meeting of the National Grand Lodge held in

the city of Memphis, Tenn., in July, 1905,
for the purpose as set forth in the preamble to
our Constitution to the end in view that new
life and enthusaism might be injected into the
Order.   Of course, through this department
a great deal of advertising is secured, but
the greater aim of the proponents of this law
was for the proper training of our youth in
the various forms of calisthenics afforded in
its training.

This department, by order of the National
Committee of Management, placed in charge
as its first major general, Brother H. J. Smith,
a man who had previous military training
and was well fitted for the task.   Through
him was added several rank divisions and also
a Ladies' Auxiliary Department.   The female
members, in several of the jurisdictions took
readily to this newly added feature and in
their later drill contests proved themselves
equal, in a great many respects, to the strict
discipline of the military.

Later heads of this department, all well
trained in the "Manual of Arms," were

Brothers W. B. Higgins, F. A. Young and
M. R. Perry, who have all contributed their
part in the building up of this work. Through
the efforts of this department, and the adver-
tisement that it has given the Order through
demonstrations, quite a few members have
been added. It has also contributed its portion
in a financial way. At the last National Grand
Lodge in 1921 the report of the Adjutant
General showed a gross collection in contributions of $27,031.02 for the four-years period.
It operates rank divisions in a total of seven
States of the national jurisdiction and is supported by an annual contribution of ten cents
per member, sixty per cent of which is given
over to the several State jurisdictions from
where the collection is derived and the balance
of forty per cent remaining in the treasury
of the national department.

This form of disbursing the funds of this
department was made law at the National
Grand Lodge held in the city of Little Rock,
Arkansas, July, 1921, upon the recommendation of the several State Grand Masters and

through it much good has been accomplished in extending the work and adding to the growth of the Order.

ADEQUATE RATE DEPARTMENT
(By J. H. McConico, Director)

The life insurance feature of most of our fraternal benefit societies came in as an after consideration. No efforts were made to secure expert advice or have the benefit certificates and premium rates figured out scientifically. The result is that the insurance departments of most of our fraternal orders have been thrown together in a kind of "catch as can" manner. The competition among our orders has been a system of increasing benefits and lowering premiums. To the informed insurance mind the results were never in doubt.

The mistakes set out above were all made by the old Friendly Societies of England and the early benefit organizations promoted by the white people of this country. When the evil days came many of them went out of business, others had to effect a reorganization

ACCOUNTING ROOM OF THE ADEQUATE RATE DIVISION

based on scientific principles. What happened to the white fraternities, is happening and will happen to the Negro fraternities. Since the Mosaic Templars of America entered the field they have been leaders in modern ideas and progressive plans. Knowing that all of our orders are going to be compelled to effect a reorganization in these insurance departments if rates are inadequate, we deemed it wisdom to start in time. Hence, in 1921 at the National Grand Lodge, we fathered a resolution authorizing the increasing of our death benefits to as high as $1,000.00. The rates to be compiled by some competent actuary. The prevailing death benefits among our Negro fraternities range from $200.00 to $300.00. These amounts were fixed some twenty years ago. The economic status of our people at that time rendered these amounts ample and satisfactory. But we have been steadily rising in the economic scale. Twenty years ago $75.00 would put up an excellent funeral for our people. Hence, $300.00 turned over to a beneficiary often made him or her independent by lifting the mortgage on the small home or farm or completing the education of the children. Three hundred dollars now will not secure a funeral. In many instances I have seen every dollar of the death benefit turned over to the undertaker and leave an unpaid balance. As we have progressed and our expenses have increased, so has come the desire for increased life insurance. Thousands of our people prefer to carry their insurance in their lodges—hence we have opened the door in the Mosaic Templars of America and it is now possible for the Negro of small means to carry a nice policy and make small monthly payments on his premium.

The resolution that authorized the creation of the Adequate Rate Department passed in 1921, but it was April, 1923, before the department was organized for business.

The writer was placed in charge of the field work of the department, Dr. J. G. Thornton, the medical end, Attorney S. A. Jones, the legal end and Acting N. G. S. and T. Mr.

A. E. Bush, the accounting.   Two experienced life insurance men, Messrs. F. A. Young
and J. G. Ish, Jr., were employed as general
agents and placed in the field.

In twelve months time more than a million
dollars worth of business has been written and
the dawn of our glory is just at hand.

Chapter V

MOSAIC CONTRIBUTIONS TO THE WORLD
WAR

On April 6, 1917, at 1:18 o'clock p. m.,
the Congress of the United States, by almost
unanimous vote, declared war against Ger-
many and the Teutonic allies. At that time
the internal conditions of this country were
by no means ideal, in so far as the Negro was
concerned, and neither were the conditions of
such that they invited 100 per cent loyalty
and morale among our group. Added to
these conditions was a well defined campaign
launched to scatter certain propaganda. The
frequency of lynching and mob violence had
in no wise abated and furnished a powerful
appeal by which it was hoped to estrange the
race. It is therefore seen that the American
Negro was confronted with a problem of such
proportions that the conservative Negro
leaders immediately saw what a crisis of this
kind would mean and they at once set about

to convince the radical element that plain duty to country and race demanded a pledge of unswerving and unquestioned loyalty.

The greatest opportunity in the history of the Mosaic Templars of America for them to show their real financial strength and worth to the nation and race then presented itself. The Order's financial worth was not only proven, but its liberal contribution in trained man-power was a fair demonstration of its potential value to the Government. This Order also furnished its proportion of conservative leaders who so valiantly beat down the fast growing propaganda and gave to members of our group such wise counsel and stern advice.

No group of people in any country, has under such trying circumstances, rallied to the call of its Government and maintained such an outstanding record as was made by the American Negro during the World's War. The Negro in every instance, pledged his support to the flag and was considered dependable in all parts of the country. His defense of the flag was of such a nature that even the appearance of a black skin was symbolic of patriotism and bravery.

He entered upon his duties not at all unmindful of the many injustices inflicted upon him, but with only one thing in mind and that was his plain duty to country. His greatest ambition was to discharge his duties as a full-fledged American citizen and gain for himself that democracy for which America theoretically stood. However, during his trials and tribulations in service overseas, still lynchings, discriminations, and the like were perpetrated against his loved ones at home. With all this, he went on and performed his duties as a citizen and continued to press his demands for that privilege and safety guaranteed him under the thirteenth, fourteenth and fifteenth amendments to the Constitution.

June 5, 1917, was the first draft call for the physically fit American male citizen between the ages of 21 and 31, and the remarkable way in which the many thousands of Negroes answered this call and accepted their tasks, quickly showed to those propagandists and other agencies the true side of his loyalty. Of course, there are many instances where the Negro was even denied this right and to the contrary were there many instances where he was illegally forced to take up arms—leaving behind dependent children and sometimes, when he himself was not physically able to discharge his duty.

Of the many millions of men drafted into service, the Negro well supplied his quota. The entire series of drafts enrolled a total number of 24,000,000 registrants between the ages of 18 and 45 years. Between the periods of June 5, 1917 (first draft) and September 12, 1918 (last draft), 21,489,470 whites had registered and 2,290,527 Negroes; we, contributing 9.63 per cent of the total draft.

The Mobilization Division of the Provost Marshal General's office furnished information as of December 16, 1918, that the total number of whites called for service under the selective draft was 2,442,586 and Negroes 367,710.

This organization, numbering its one hundred thousand members, saw its opportunity to do for its race and Government. Knowing, with a membership of one hundred thousand (and that this meant control of practically a half a million (500,000) colored Americans) that much good could be done, the officials of the organization spared no time in acting at such an opportune time. With the previous training, through Manual of Arms, given our Uniform Rank Department, which gave to those young men a decided advantage, the work in this particular division was accelerated and all of the Rank Divisions throughout the jurisdiction were requested to begin intensive training. The Mosaic Templars of America at that time had upon its roll of members 29,486 persons of draft age who willingly signed the registration cards and took up arms. As a result we furnished quite a number of commissioned and non-commissioned officers, as well as privates, who were well scattered in the various divisions of the army from stevedores and members of the labor battalions to ranking officers of the Medical Corps. Our women also readily responded to the colors as Red Cross Nurses, Y. W. C. A. workers, Social Welfare workers, and the like. In fact, our group was well represented in every phase and activity of the war, and our services were invaluable.

During the enlistment of those members of the Mosaic Templars of America in the draft age and who had actually been pressed into service, the officials, strained every nerve to lend all possible aid to the Government. Without request or demand, they most willingly made provisions to exempt those who were drafted from the payment of dues and taxations and in the event of death while in service their beneficiaries would receive the full amount of the proceeds of their policies and all other benefits that are usually given. Such patriotic actions on the part of the officials gained the immediate notice and whole hearted endorsement of the membership, and too, quite a number of persons not identified with the Order made complimentary mention.

The membership of the organization felt it their duty to "do their bit" and consequently, a fund was started and styled as "Patriotic Fund." This fund was supervised by the officials of the Order and was made up through free-will offerings from the membership, such moneys being contributed toward helping to reimburse the Endowment Department in the exemption of the regular dues and taxations of those male members who had been called to active service. At the termination of the war the collections for this fund were discontinued. The moral effect, both upon the membership and public, was sweeping and gave a great deal of encouragement to our "boys in the trenches."

LIBERTY LOAN DRIVES

Not only did we, as an organization, make the supreme sacrifice in giving our loved ones, but those on the second line of defense augmented this most willingly, cheerfully, and liberally by giving to the nation's call for

VOUCHER CHECK

J. E. BUSH

NATIONAL GRAND SCRIBE MOSAIC TEMPLARS OF AMERICA

NOTICE
If any part of this check is detached it is void and must not be paid. If any portion names below are unknown the Banker must require Guardianship papers, and require the Guardian to sign on behalf of the minors.

October 2nd 1917   No. 11149

UPON THE PAYEE EXECUTING IN INK THE RECEIPT ON BACK OF THIS VOUCHER CHECK

On demand   **Pay to the order of**

Hon. W. G. McAdoo Sec'y of Treasury

$50,000⁰⁰

FIFTY THOUSAND DOLLARS   **Dollars**

To ENGLAND NATIONAL BANK,
LITTLE ROCK, ARK.

81-15

By J. E. Bush
National Grand Scribe, M. T. A.

MAKE ALL ENDORSEMENTS BELOW

Received this amount stated in this Voucher-Check in full payment of the within account.

W. McAdoo Payee
Sec'y of the Treasury Payee

Payee

Payee

Payee

VOUCHER CHECK

J. E. BUSH

NATIONAL GRAND SCRIBE MOSAIC TEMPLARS OF AMERICA

NOTICE
If any part of this check is detached it is void and must not be paid. If any portion names hereon are unknown the Banker must require Guardianship papers, and require the Guardian to sign on behalf of the minors.

May 21-1918   No. 11148

UPON THE PAYEE EXECUTING IN INK THE RECEIPT ON BACK OF THIS VOUCHER CHECK

On demand   **Pay to the order of**

England National Bank

$32000⁰⁰

THIRTY TWO THOUSAND DOLLARS   **Dollars**

To ENGLAND NATIONAL BANK,
LITTLE ROCK, ARK.

81-15

By J. E. Bush
National Grand Scribe, M. T. A.

financial aid. The exact amount given by our group may never be ascertained, but we are safe in saying that we gave way up in the millions, and gave unstintingly and with an open pocket.

The Mosaic Templars of America gained nation-wide attention and considerable press mention in buying liberally of the five loan campaigns and also of the War Savings Stamp drive. The first purchase was made June 1, 1917, for an amount of $18,000.00. The second October 20, 1917, for $50,000.00. The third May 21,, 1918, for $32,000.00; fourth October 19, 1918, for $10,000.00; fifth April 22, 1919, for $15,000.00; making a total of $125,000.00 subscribed and paid in cash. These investments were considered gilt-edged and yielded a safe return, but the mere monetary return was only an after consideration. The thought uppermost in the minds of those engineering the purchases was to first answer the country's call. Secondly, to influence those in authority that equality and justice be meted out to those Negro men who so

unselfishly served the colors in such a crisis.
Both our National and State officials played
very important roles in answering the call for
"minute men" speakers during these financial
campaigns, so well did they do their work
during the Victory Loan drive, that several
were awarded medals as tokens of thanks and
esteem for their valuable services.

The part that the Mosaic Templars of
America played, as a whole, in contributing
freely of her sons and daughters, most assur-
edly carried out the traditions of its race and
distinguished itself for loyalty and patriotism.
The organization is now freely referred to in
press and speech for this enviable record of
service to the race and Government.

Chapter VI

WORTH TO THE RACE

As noted in an earlier chapter, when the Mosaic Templars were first conceived it was intended to fill the local need of the community. The founders could not see at that time the possibility of its expansion. The founders were young men, young in experience as well as age. Coincident with growth in age, came growth in experience, not only in the lodge work but in the race's problem.

Mr. Bush, having leadership of his immediate group thrust upon him, saw at once that the crying need of the people was to weld them in a great constructive and co-operative force. The organized lodge gave him the best foundation for this purpose. While the need for caring for the sick and the burial of the dead was the prime factor in calling into existence the organization, Mr. Bush was quick to recognize that the dominant need was to prepare the race to live. Politically and economically the weakest link in the upward

trend of the race was its utter lack of race con-
sciousness and racial solidarity. Being convinced that this was the pressing need, the
accomplishment of the same became one of
the objectives of the Order.

One of the cardinal tenets of the organization is brotherhood. This principle became
the background of the larger purpose which
had become possible. Mr. Bush had always
been an exponent of the brotherhood idea.
He saw all around him his brethren in the
slavery of ignorance, disease, superstition and
distrust of each other. He realized that the
fate of one could be the fate of all; that we
have always been unescapably involved in a
common destiny, and since man has never
been able to separate himself from another's
wrong or woe, that we cannot escape brotherhood of some kind, therefore it was his immediate task to promote a co-operative brotherhood, with all the fruits which would come
from such a spirit.

The instant success attending the broaden-
ing of the scope of the work of the Order, con-

vinced all that co-operation was good and competition bad, that the race would most surely flourish through mutual aid and mutual understanding.

The organization reversed the old-time saying that competition is the life of trade by substituting co-operation for competition.

There is no race organizaion that has taught more effectively, by concrete example, that co-operation was one of the most powerful cogs in the wheel of racial success.

THE MOSAICS STRENGTHEN RACE CONFIDENCE

From the day of Emancipation down to the present the trail of racial progress has been strewn with the wrecks of misplaced confidence and incompetent leadership. In our commercial and fraternal enterprises we suffered as much from incompetency as we did from dishonesty. We were virtually children in the wilderness and it took the wisdom and courage of a modern Moses to lead us out.

Confidence of the masses of the race was at low ebb, in this they did not deserve severe

censure. Their confidence had been abused
from every angle. They had been the easy
prey of every designing self-styled leader of
their own race and of the demagogue of the
opposite race. The leaders of the organization saw that the most important step to be
taken was to build up this waning confidence.

Mr. Bush had determined to have the confidence of the race in itself, restored and that
this could be done only through wise leadership and an unbending virtue, without selfiish
ambition.

With the sure sagacity of a leader of men,
he selected a little group of tried and true men
and with this little group, entered into a com-
pact that through their entire course, sink or
swim, live or die, that their organization
should never betray the confidence of their
people. Mr. Bush was the head, the heart and
the conscience of the movement. He met
many obstacles. At the first show of success,
the birds of prey hovered around, itching
palms were often displayed rather than "My
heart and my hand," but he stood resolute

REV. D. McQUEEN
State Grand Master of Nebraska.

Born December 11, 1868, in San Marcus, Hays County, Tex.

Elected State Grand Master of Nebraska June 22, 1921, at Omaha, Neb.

Approximate number of lodges when elected, 7.

Approximate number of members when elected, 170.

Present number of lodges, 11.

Present number of members, 728.

Connected with Order 5 years.

DR. G. W. WEST
State Grand Master of North Carolina.

Born January 16, 1883, at Butte, Mont.

Elected State Grand Master at the Grand Lodge held at Winston Salem, October 19, 1920.

Approximate number of lodges when elected, 60.

Approximate number of members when elected, 2,100.

Present number of lodges, 92.

Present number of members, 3,325.

Connected with the Order 5 years.

and undismayed. Without a chart, without a beacon, he guided his organization safely through storm and darkness. He held his steadfast way, like the sun across the firmament and upon a searching survey there has been no act of the leaders or their successors in this great organization, that any member of the race would deplore or reverse.

The success of the Mosaic Templars was contagious. It has been reflected in many phases of Negro life, individually and collectively, not only in Arkansas, but throughout the United States and in foreign lands.

The organization has added stimulus to racial effort not only along fraternal lines, but in co-operative enterprises.

The organization with its vast resources, while jealously guarding its assets, has always come to the rescue of distressed business enterprises, when it would be shown that the investment was safe. Thousands of farms and homes of members of the organization have been saved from going under the hammer.

In its efforts to be a benefactor to the race

it has encountered its difficulties. It has attempted to teach self-reliance, individual independence, and not pauperize anyone. Many who were in the organization for the "Loaves and fishes" have been troublesome when request for help had been refused. Each application for a loan or for charity undergoes a most searching investigation by a committee of competent officials before definite action is taken. Those whose applications are deemed unworthy are rejected, and these unworthy applicants usually become disgruntled and say harsh things about the Order. This has not deterred the officials from their committed policy, and no worthy appeal goes unheeded.

Colored people find it much harder to get backing, from financial organizations and banks, than do other groups. We are yet weak in banks of our own. The organization as far as its resources will permit, his filled a large portion of this existing gap in the racial need.

ITS INFLUENCE IN CITY AND STATE

Little Rock justly boasts of the splendid feeling existing between the races in this city as contrasted with many other Southern cities. It is not an extravagant boast to say that nothing has contributed more to the cordial relations existing between the races than the Mosaic Templars of America. All the citizens of Little Rock, irrespective of race, take pride in claiming the organization as one of the great enterprises of the city and State. Whenever friction occurs or when movements are begun inimical to the race's interest, the Mosaic Templars' representatives are sure to get respectful hearing.

Much of the prosperity of the city is attributed to the Mosaics. There is no business organization in the city enjoying more confidence among banks than does this organization.

A TRAINING SCHOOL FOR YOUNG PEOPLE

There is no organization under the direct control of colored people that gives more employment to the young people of the race than does the Mosaic Templars of America. Around the general headquarters there are employed nearly one hundred young persons, mostly young women.

Some years ago the opportunity for business courses was very limited for colored youth, and it was through the opportunity to work in the several departments of the Order that many of our young people have been taught to become splendid office clerks and these young people are in demand throughout the country.

In the subdivisions of the general department trained experts are secured as heads of these divisions and the clerks employed work under their direction. Efficiency and merit are the basis of promotion. The business system employed by the Mosaics is such that other organizations and business interests are always glad to secure their help from among those who have received their training under the Mosaic business administration.

Aside from those employed in the general headquarters, the several State jurisdictions give employment to hundreds of others in clerical capacity. The field force of deputy organizers give employment to hundreds of men and women who find this a lucrative field of endeavor.

The organization has triumphed in its major undertaking. Begging or soliciting funds with which to bury the dead has become an obsolete custom wherever the Mosaics have set up an organization, and the country is honeycombed with their temples and chambers. The entire success cannot be measured by what the Mosaics have done alone, but it must be measured by the influence it has had on similar organizations which are emulating their example.

The Mosaics have been accepted as a pattern for many new fraternities who strive to conduct their business along the splendid lines laid down by the Order.

The Mosaics were among the first to create a secret order on original work by the race. Its signs, grips, passwords and ritualistic work are all original Negro products, and they have never been called into court to prove their right and title to use the same.

Chapter VII

BIOGRAPHICAL SKETCHES OF LEADING OFFICIALS OF THE ORDER

It is regretted that owing to the limited space in this volume that it will be impossible to give full mention of the many faithful and loyal officers who are now in their various stations rendering yeoman service in the Order. There can be found no more loyal and devoted group of officials in any organization than can be found in the various State jurisdictions.

They are loyal to the core and never sulk in their tents. The present story could not be told if these men and women had not contributed their bit. In every community where the lodge exists they have enshrined their memory in the hearts of thousands. The weather has never been too cold, the downpour of rain too heavy, the darkness too intense or the danger too great for these ministering angels, true disciples of the teachings of the Order, that they could not be found going where duty called.

REV. J. A. DAVIS
PAST NATIONAL GRAND MASTER

They have carried the true Mosaic enthusiasm. They have trampled over prejudice and
opposition with nothing more than their faith
in themselves, in the race and in the Order.

Their zeal and enthusiasm spread like con-
tagion and has permeated the whole racial fab-
ric. Too much in the way of commendation
cannot be said in behalf of this army of earnest
men and women who have done and who are
doing much for the carrying on of the Order.

The following biographies contain much
of an inspirational nature and is given as mer-
ited tribute to these men and women who are
at the helm steering the Order to surer and
greater heights. In the years that are to follow some one will, through speech or pen,
give just estimate and due tribute for which
space will not here permit.

JOHN ABRAHAM DAVIS

The Rev. J. A. Davis enjoys the unique
distinction of being the only surviving charter
member of the organization. He has been
actively identified with the Mosaics from their
beginning and at present enjoys the coveted

distinction of being one of the Past National Grand Masters, an honorary title bestowed for meritorious service.

He is a native of this State, having been born at Center Point in 1848. He came to Little Rock in 1862 and secured work as a Government teamster. He was quite small for his age and only by his insistence did he overcome the wagon master's doubts about his ability to handle a six-mule team and was given a trial. He served with entire satisfaction and soon established a reputation as being one of the most dependable men in this service. This work gave him a taste for army life and he enlisted as a private in the cavalry service of the army. His company was detailed for frontier service and he had an exciting career as a soldier.

He was with Custer in his campaigns against the Cheyenne Indians and had many hairbreadth escapes. He rose to the rank of sergeant and after five years' service was honorably discharged. He is now on the pension rolls of the Government.

Returning to Little Rock, different from most army men, he united with Bethel A. M. E. Church under the pastorate of the Rev. P. W. Wade, who in later years became a most prominent minister of that connection. Some years later feeling that he was "called" to preach, he was licensed as a local preacher under the late Rev. H. C. Beasley and continues active in the ministry.

At the beginning of the Organization he was made National Grand Treasurer and filled this position most creditably for thirty-three years until the combining of this office with the National Grand Scribe's office.

As Treasurer of the organization, he was not content to fill this position alone, but during a period of thirty-seven years he has been active on the field in Arkansas. He has been a successful organizer and there are several lodges in the State named in honor of him.

He has reached the ripe age of seventy-six years and is still vigorous and aggressive. It can really be said of him that he is seventy-six years young.

BRIEF SKETCH OF THE REV. S. J. ELLIOTT,
NATIONAL GRAND MASTER

The Rev. S. J. Elliott, present National Grand Master, was born July 16, 1855, in the little town of Hillsboro, Alabama. He spent his early life on a farm with his parents, Anderson and Joana Elliott. As soon as he was old enough his parents sent him to the little school in Hillsboro, where he attended, at various intervals, until 1875. In June of 1875 he was married to Miss Leah Jones and enjoyed a happy married life for thirty-two years, when his devoted wife and companion was called by death. From this union fifteen children were born.

In 1873 he was converted in a great revival which swept through the little town of Hillsboro, and united with the C. M. E. Church. From his early youth he had always exhibited a deep spiritual attitude and within two years after uniting with the church, he was licensed to preach. This was in September, 1875, and from that time up to the present he has been active in the ministry of his denomina-

S. J. ELLIOTT

NATIONAL GRAND MASTER

tion. By reason of his devotion to the cause
for which he had consecrated himself, his rise
in the church was rapid. In 1878 he was admitted to the Alabama Conference, held in
Auburn, and served in the pastorate until
1891, when he was made presiding elder by
Bishop L. H. Holsey and he served in this
capacity until 1914, when he was drafted by
the Mosaic Templars of America to serve in
the exalted position which he now holds. As
a minister, he served with credit in high positions in annual and in general conferences, and
notwithstanding his manifold duties as National Grand Master he never fails to meet his
Annual Conference in Alabama and the General Conference of the church. Some time
after the death of his devoted wife, he married
Mis Eva O. Avery in 1910, and this has
proved a happy union. She is a devoted wife
and is a helpmeet in every sense of the term.

AS A MOSAIC

Mr. Elliott became a Mosaic in 1904, joining Key of the West Chamber at Talledega,
Alabama, which Chamber was presided over

by Mrs. Anna Strickland, an enthusiastic Mosaic, who did much to promote the Order in Alabama, in its early existence in that State.

It was characteristic of Mr. Elliott to do with all his might whatever he entered into, and after one year in the Order, by reason of his excellent work as a member in the ranks, he was made Deputy Grand Master by G. W. Mitchell, who was at that time Grand Master of Alabama. In the same year he was named delegate to the National Grand Lodge meeting which was held in Memphis, Tenn. In this national meeting he made a speech in defending the national organization against an attack by a disgruntled delegate. This speech attracted the favorable attention of Mr. Keatts and Mr. Bush, and as there was an impending vacancy in the position of Grand Master in Alabama, Mr. Keatts offered the position to Mr. Elliott. Owing to the illness of his wife, Mr. Elliott was prevented from attending the Grand Lodge meeting in Alabama. He saw the Grand Mastership go to another, but in this can be seen the hand of destiny. If he had been made Grand Master of Alabama, he would not have been made National Aaronic, which is equivalent to Vice-National Grand Master, and being National Aaronic, he automatically became National Grand Master at the death of the lamented Alexander.

The present high position, in the Order, which he occupies was not the result of favor bestowed, but it came to him indirectly as the reward of faithful and efficient service from the humblest position in the ranks, working ever upward. Many men having attained the rank and position which he held in his church and the reputation which he had made for himself would not have been willing to go from the lower rungs of the ladder, slowly, but surely, upward.

In the first Grand Lodge held under the administration of William Alexander, for Alabama, Mr. Elliott was appointed to the humble position of agent for the Mosaic Guide, the official paper of the Order. He served so satisfactorily for two years, that he was promoted to the position of Grand Lecturer for

Alabama. He held this position for four years, serving two of these years without pay and the remaining two he received the small pay of $25.00 per year. From this position he was elected, in the Grand Lodge meeting held at Montgomery, to the position of Chief Grand Deputy for Alabama, serving in this capacity only three months. At this same meeting he was named Fraternal Delegate to the Grand Lodges of Louisiana and Arkansas. He was further honored by his Grand Lodge by being sent to the dedication exercises of the National Grand Temple building at Little Rock. This Temple was the crowning triumph of the Alexander administration and consummation of the dream of Mr. Bush. This occasion had brought together in Little Rock, race leaders from all parts of the country. The dedicatory address was delivered by the late Dr. Booker T. Washington, intimate friend of Dr. Elliott.

It was at this meeting that he was selected as National Aaronic Grand Master. This position was considered by many, just an empty honor and would be the last place sought by those with ambition. But true to his spirit of unquestioned obedience to superior authority, he accepted the place, little dreaming that in seven days, through the tragedy of death he would become the head of the Order. On the 30th day of November, 1913, all that was mortal of Alexander fell a victim of an assassin's mad act. Elliott automatically became National Grand Master and was duly installed in this office December 3, 1913, by L. L. Powell, State Grand Master of Alabama. Since that time he has been consecutively elected to succeed himself.

His rise to the highest place within the Order, an organization that has commanded the admiration of the world, as a fraternity, has not changed him one iota. He is still the modest, unassuming, broadhearted Christian gentleman, generous to a fault. During the life of Mr. Bush when they were associated officials it is not recorded that there was ever a breach of faith beween the two.

In his annual report to the National Grand
Lodge held at Tuskegee Institute, Alabama,
July, 1914, the National Grand Scribe, J. E.
Bush, paid the following tribute to Dr. El-
liott:

As already stated, after the assassination of Brother
William Alexander, Brother S. J. Elliott of Decatur,
Alabama, then acting National Aaronic Grand
Master, became National Grand Master. I find him
to be a Christian gentleman, a hard worker, and an
honest and faithful man. He, too, like Brother Alexander, cannot be classed by the college-bred student
as an educated man, but he seems to be well up in
all the details that would be required of a man to
manage an organization like the National Order of
the Mosaic Templars of America. Since his inaugur-
ation as National Grand Master he has brought into
the Order such great men as Bishop Clinton, Bishop
Carter, and a host of others. He, too, has worked
day and night to encourage and build up the membership of the Order. His energy, pluck and zeal
for the organization has caused to be added to its
membership during his eight months of administration 8,480 members and 274 lodges, something like
more than one lodge for every day that he has been
National Grand Master. Mr. Alexander assisted very
materially in erecting a temple at Little Rock, Arkansas, at a cost of $60,000.00. This temple will
act as a monument for the Mosaic Templars of
America in particular and the race in general, and
Mr. Alexander's name will be cherished and honored

WASH JORDAN
NATIONAL CHIEF GRAND DEPUTY

as long as this building stands. We loaned to the Temple fund during the lifetime of Mr. Alexander $45,000.00, and at his death our surplus (cash) on that account had sunk to $35,214.85. Notwithstanding Mr. Elliott has been Grand Master only eight months, this cash surplus, not counting the loan of $45,000.00, is now $68,662.34. We are, therefore, proud of Mr. Elliott as a man, proud of him as a Christian gentleman, and proud of him for the good work that he has done since becoming National Grand Master. We therefore recommend that he be re-elected and given a man's chance. Nothing less could be asked, nothing more will be expected. All hail the name of S. J. Elliott.

WASH JORDAN, NATIONAL CHIEF GRAND DEPUTY

Wash Jordan was born in Moscow, Mississippi, January 22, 1874. He was the tenth child of his parents. It is evident that his parents did not subscribe to "race suicide," as thirteen more children were born. Early in the boy's life his parents removed to Arkansas for economical reasons. His father was an indefatigable worker and notwithstanding the incumbrance of a large family, from his savings earned as a railroad shop worker he was able to purchase a little home for his family. The pace he set as a hard worker was too much for him, he became broken in health and for many years remained an invalid. Wash, being the eldest in the family had to assume the man's part and found it necessary to leave school in the seventh grade. He secured work at a brickyard and earned sufficient to provide fairly well for the family. Leaving the brickyard he secured work at a large grocery store, starting in the humble position as porter he worked up to the top and was made city drummer for the firm, a distinction that no other colored man ever enjoyed in Little Rock.

He had always been ambitious to be his own boss and by exercising the utmost economy he was able in a few years to launch out in business for himself. He became proprietor of a tailoring company under the firm name of "Jordan and Collins." He built up a lucrative business in this line, but chafing under the restraint of an indoor life an opportunity came to sell at a good margin of

profit and he embarked in the real estate business. He enjoys the reputation of having sold
and secured more homes for colored people in
Little Rock than any other man.

Characteristic of Mr. Bush, young Jordan's
activity and success did not escape his observ-
ing eye, and he soon had him enlisted in the
rank of Mosaic builders. With his usual energy he entered into this work. He had to
win his spurs, nothing came from Mr. Bush
on a silver platter, you had to win your place.
Mr. Jordan went in determined to win.

He was made State Grand Deputy of Arkansas, his future promotion was left in his
own hands. The National Department offered as a prize, the National Chief Grand
Deputyship to the State Deputy who organized the greatest number of lodges. At the
national meeting in Tuskegee, against the
field, Wash Jordan was easily the winner of
the coveted position, which was awarded him
at this meeting and which he is now filling.

He has held this place for ten years and has
added thousands of members to the organiza-

tion, a number of Temples, Chambers and Palaces and has commissioned a score of deputies.

He has served as State Grand Master for the following jurisdictions: Oklahoma, Michigan, New Jersey and North Carolina. And he has remained at the head of organizations in these States until they were built up sufficiently strong to organize their own Grand Lodges.

There is no man connected with the Order who enjoys a wider range of acquaintance with the membership than Wash Jordan.

In 1900 he led to the altar Miss Annie P. Johnson, who was one of Little Rock's accomplished women. Two sons were born from this union. Her death which occurred nine years later was a severe shock to him. His second wife, Miss Ruth Duncan of Plumerville, Arkansas, has proven a wonderful aid to him in his work, acting for a long while as his private secretary. She became so proficient in her work and knew every detail so well that he found it possible to leave the details

SCIPIO A. JONES
NATIONAL ATTORNEY GENERAL

of the office entirely to her keeping and spend more of his time on the field in active organization. Mr. Jordan is one of the very useful men connected with the organization in high official capacity.

SCIPIO A. JONES, NATIONAL ATTORNEY GENERAL

Scipio Africanus Jones, General Attorney for the Mosaic Templars of America and nationally known famous lawyer, is pre-eminently one of the oustanding figures in public life today. Born and reared in Arkansas, recognizing no material barriers, and overcoming the handicap of prejudice and discrimination, Scipio A. Jones has risen from an obscure lawyer of the Southwest to a pinnacle of fame and national prominence rarely attained by many men under so adverse circumstances. His whole professional career has been altruistically devoted to the protection of the inalienable rights of his own people and his entire life has been spent in safeguarding the legal rights of Negroes in a section of the United States where fearlessness and the courage of his convictions are a Negro lawyer's most needed adjuncts to intrinsic ability and superior knowledge of the law.

He was admitted to the Pulaski County Circuit Court and began the practice of law at a period when the numerous facilities that now smooth the path of the lawyer were not so well known. It was no easy task to become a lawyer in those days, especially a Negro, and it required no common share of industry and perseverance. But Scipio Jones was born with that inherent gift of commonsense—the first condition of success—and the power that all men of high practical capacity have. Modestly he approached the bar devoid of any mercenary motives, but inspired with an exalted ideal of service to his fellow man. As it has been truly said that a lawyer has a large opportunity to shape the course of others in the conduct of life, more than this, to help shape that of the whole community, it can be truly said then that Scipio Jones has played a very important part in helping to shape the conduct of life in the community in which he has lived and worked all his life.

It was not long before he began to attract the attention of the bar by the skillful handling of his cases so as to capture both the judge and the jury. His quiet, unostentatious, and reserved demeanor won for him the esteem and admiration of his contemporaries; and his simple logic, clever and convincing manner of argument and presentation of facts in a case before the jury marked him instantly as one of the most brilliant jurists of that day. His practice soon became very extensive and his influence was simultaneously aroused to the problems affecting the welfare of the race. Although a lawyer by profession, he was, also, necessarily a student of economic and sociologic conditions of the Negroes in Arkansas and by reason thereof, he identified himself with those agencies and humanitarian projects which were started for the amelioration of the conditions that were retarding the progress of the Negroes in all fields of human endeavor. Thus he made the profession of law his life investment, and, like any other investment called for prudence and judgment if failure was to be averted and success assured.

He rapidly triumphed over the adverse conditions of his early years because nature had bestowed upon him high and rare powers. On November 26, 1900, he was admitted to the Supreme Court of Arkansas and on October 30, 1901, to the United States District Court for the Western Division of the Eastern District of Arkansas. His rise as a lawyer was marked by a series of brilliant legal victories. His first local achievement as a member of the bar was the successful fight that he waged against the pernicious county convict farm-lease system in force at one time in Arkansas. By this system the county farms were leased to contract lessees. Both white and colored prisoners were sentenced to these farms for twenty-five dollars and costs and while there were allowed only fifty cents a day when they worked, and charged for each day that they lost. Prisoners at the end of six months would owe as much as they did when they

were first sent to the farm.   Judge Jones'
fearless fight against this system and in behalf
of those unfortunate people caused the court
to rule that all prisoners sent to the county
farms were entitled to seventy-five cents a day
whether they worked or not.   His personal
interest and sympathy in humanitarian problems and in the sociologic conditions of the
unfortunate members of society won for him
a warm place in the hearts of the common
people, of whom Lincoln said, "God must
love the common people, for He made so many
of them."   A leader in civic affairs and out-
spoken exponent of the political rights of
Negroes in Arkansas, Judge Jones soon distinguished himself politically by his victory
against that insidious piece of legislation
familiarly known in the South as "the grandfather clause."   It was through his political
strategy that the white people of Arkansas
were defeated in their efforts to have adopted
to the Constitution of Arkansas that in-
famous amendment which would have dis-
franchised every Negro voter in the State of

Arkansas. In May, 1905, Judge Jones was
admitted to the Supreme Court of the United
States and on December 10, 1914, to the
United States Court of Appeals. He was
elected special judge in the Municipal Court
of Little Rock, Arkansas, April 8, 1915, and
served in that capacity with distinction and
credit.

He shaped his legal career in a period that
was epochal in Negro history and whatever
material progress that the Negroes of Arkansas have achieved, Judge Jones has largely
been responsible for a great deal of it.
At that time the Negroes all over the South
were awakening from their lethargic state and
were beginning to launch forth into diversi-
fied business enterprises that marked the initial
efforts of our people into the commercial
world. Notably among these many enterprises were the fraternal beneficiary societies
which were experiencing the vicissitudes of
development so common to such organizations. The Mosaic Templars of America,
now the Gibraltar of Negro fraternal benefi-

ciary societies in America, were stretching out into other sections of the country and were beginning to grow so rapidly that the late John E. Bush, the founder and genius of the Order, readily realized the necessity of calling into the inner circle, a man who was possessed of superior legal attainments and qualifications to help shape the policies of the Order. In Scipio A. Jones, Mr. Bush immediately recognized those qualities of the trained counsel which he was seeking. Judge Jones by dint of hard work, concentration, and enthusiasm had slowly but surely forged to the forefront as the legal genius of the Negroes in Arkansas and his intellectual honesty, hospitality to truth and integrity had attracted the attention of Mr. Bush. The linking together of two keen business minds as possessed by Mr. Bush and Judge Jones has been primarily responsible for the remarkably solid and substantial growth of the Mosaic Templars of America. And no better criterion can be found of the legal genius of Judge Jones than the efficient and highly competent

manner in which all the legal problems affecting the Order have been so capably handled by him. As legal principles constitute
the bedrock foundation upon which all business structures stand, the Mosaics owe their
solid foundation and successful operation to
the circumspective formulation of laws governing the Order by Judge Jones. During the
great war, Judge Jones was frequently con-
sulted, not only by the officials of the Government, but also by the leaders of most of
the fraternal orders in the State for his advice in regard to their purchase of Liberty
Loan Bonds, War Saving Stamps and other
Government securities. No greater tribute
can be paid to Judge Jones' patriotism than
to quote from his speech to the National
Grand Lodge of the Mosaics at the outbreak
of the war:

These are perilous times. Among those who will
march under the flag of the United States, will be true
and tried Mosaics. These Mosaics will leave their
families, to fight and die for you and for me.
Your Executive Committee bought $30,000.00
worth of Liberty Loan Bonds, but we ought to go
further, as "the end is not yet." If you can't fight

with your musket, you can fight with your dollars.
There are no cowards among us—no slackers on our
rolls.

Mr. W. G. McAdoo, on his itinerary
through the South during one of the intensive
campaigns for the sale of Liberty bonds paid
a visit to Little Rock, where he delivered an
address. On this occasion, Judge Jones, as
General Attorney for the Mosaics, purchased
$50,000.00 worth of Liberty Bonds and he
had the especial honor of personally tendering
to Mr. McAdoo a check for this amount.
Judge Jones was also honored during the war
by the late Woodrow Wilson, then President,
who appointed him as Associate Member of
the Legal Advisory Board for Pulaski
County. He was also chairman of the drive
for the United Charities and under his supervision $143,000.00 was raised in ten days.
His indefatigable efforts in behalf of the Government in its prosecution of the great war
won for him many encomiums.

His main legal achievement and one that
brought him into the limelight, not only na-

tionally, but also internationally, was his masterly and dexterous handling of the famous Elaine case. His conduct of this case has stamped him as one of the greatest trial lawyers in this country. From December, 1919, when he first went down to the hotbed of prejudice and hatred — Helena, Arkansas, where it took iron nerve to go in so critical a time, to defend those twelve unfortunate Negroes, to 1923, when the Supreme Court of the United States handed down the decision reversing the conviction of six of the riot victims, Judge Jones stood at the forefront during those four long years in which the most bitterly fought legal battles in this country took place. Never before in the history of the United States were trials conducted in an atmosphere of hatred, intimidation, coercion, hostility and prejudice as those Elaine trials. The most eminent jurists of this country assert that the Elaine trials were the greatest legal battles in the history of the United States. Mr. Louis Marshall, noted lawyer, called the decision of the Supreme Court of the

United States, *"A great achievement in Con-
stitutional law."* Another legal victory of
national interest and importance to the credit
of Judge Jones was that of the Arkansas Colored Shriners case. In several of the Southern
States white Shriners had brought injunctions
to restrain the colored Shriners from operating
as such and to prevent them from wearing
the Shriners' pins, fezzes, and regalia. The
only case won by the Colored Shriners in the
South was the one in Arkansas, where Judge
Jones was the attorney in the case; in all the
others the Colored Shriners lost. Judge Jones
was also one of the leading counsel in the
famous Pythian case in Arkansas in which the
Insurance Commissioner of Arkansas sought
to put out of business the Grand Lodge of
the Knights of Pythias, Arkansas Jurisdiction. The Insurance Commissioner lost the
case in the lower court, appealed it to the Supreme Court where the decision of the lower
court was affirmed.

It would require a whole book to record
the many notable achievements of Judge Jones

and his multifarious activities throughout the
State.   Aside from his enormously large private practice he has always taken an active
part in all civic movements looking toward
the betterment of Negroes in Arkansas and the
Southwest.   Politically he has been the potential leader for years and is today the foremost
Negro political leader in the State of Arkansas.   In 1908 and in 1912 he was a delegate
to the National Republican Convention and
has from time to time participated in numerous important Republican councils.   In addition to being the General Counsel for the Mosaics, he is the General Attorney for the Inter-
national Order of Twelve, Knights and
Daughters of Tabor, the Royal Circle of
Friends of the World; State Attorney for the
Order of Eastern Star, Household of Ruth,
Masonic Benefit Association, and for the
Grand Court of Calanthe.   He is also Chairman of the Board of the Peoples Ice and Fuel
Company, the only Negro ice company in
the United States that has constructed its own
ice plant at the cost of $120,000.00; Chair-

man of the Board of Managers of the Aged and Orphans' Industrial Home, located at Dexter, Arkansas, whose existence today is due largely to the untiring efforts of Judge Jones in raising sufficient funds for the maintenance of this charitable institution. And he is now in charge of a campaign to raise enough funds to make the institution self-supporting. He is never too busy to lend a helping hand to any worthy cause and his advice is constantly sought on all matters affecting the race in Arkansas. He stands out as the acknowledged leader in Arkansas and receives the endorsement of the people in this capacity for his integrity. Though his professional career may not have proved an investment of the highest and richest returns, financially, it certainly has intellectually, socially and morally. Esteemed, honored, and loved by both races, Judge Jones has still many more years of fruitful service before him and will yet add many laurels to his crown.

JOHN HAMILTON M'CONICO, NATIONAL
AUDITOR

One of the most active and most valuable
men to the organization is J. H. McConico.

He was born in the little town of Living-
ston, Alabama, where he spent the earlier
years of his life. He enjoyed better advantages
than the average boy of his period. He came
from a family noted for their natural ability.
Though his parents had been slaves, they were
fortunate in enjoying superior advantages
over the usual life of a slave. His grandfather
belonged to that peculiar type of unlettered
but powerful group of ante-bellum preachers
who were the acknowledged leaders of their
people. He was one of the first to plant the
great A. M. E. Zion Church in the State of
Alabama, and was one of the most influential
preachers in that church, during his day. His
father followed in the footsteps of the grandfather and was one of the prominent ministers
of the Zion Church.

His parents were determined to give their
son every advantage that had been denied

J. H. McCONICO
NATIONAL GRAND AUDITOR

them in securing an education, and as soon as he had completed the course offered in the public school of his home town, he was sent to the A. and M. College located at Normal, Alabama. The president of this institution, the brilliant and well known educator, the late W. H. Council, soon observed the unusual ability of young McConico and became personally interested in him and a close intimacy sprang up between the president and the young student, quite unusual to pupil and president. Mr. McConico found himself enjoying the confidence of the president to such a degree that for a long time, assisting in classroom work and the discipline of the boys, he was known as the "student professor."

Throughout his college career he maintained a high record for scholarship and was one of the honor graduates, delivering one of the addresses on commencement day, the "red letter" day of all days. Young as he was, his address made a profound impression on the older heads who predicted for the young man a brilliant future. What he has accomplished since leaving college has not fallen short of their prediction.

Directly upon graduation he went to Atlanta, Georgia, where he was employed as foreman on the Atlanta Appeal, a leading publication owned by C. H. J. Taylor, who served as Recorder of Deeds, under the Cleveland administration.

McConico's natural bent and inclination was the newspaper field and to satisfy this craving, at his first opportunity, he launched out in business for himself. Returning to his home he began the publication of a paper called The Advance. This venture, like most colored papers, had its ups and downs and while the work satisfied his cravings, he had to forego the unequal struggle for financial reasons. His friend and benefactor, Professor Council, still interested in the young man, called him to come to Normal and accept a place on the faculty. When President Joseph A. Booker needed a man of special training for a place in Arkansas Baptist College, he applied to Normal and the president sent him

the name of McConico. He accepted work in
the Arkansas Baptist College, at Little Rock,
and continued a member of the faculty for
two years. But nothing could keep him out
of the newspaper game. He purchased a half
interest in the Little Rock Reporter which was
owned by W. A. Singfield, who is now a
prominent member of the Little Rock bar.
Mr. McConico threw all of his energy into
this new venture and soon had this paper up
to a high plane of journalism.

At the launching of the now defunct Capitol City Bank, he was made assistant cashier
and notwithstanding the misfortunes which
later overtook this enterprise, he had made a
most excellent executive. The closing of the
bank made the future for the young man exceedingly gloomy, but his self-confidence
never deserted him. He met the issues bravely
and bore up under a load that would have
carried down the average young man. Those
men of the race that knew character and ability, never lost confidence in or questioned the
integrity of young McConico. He was

asked to take the management of the Arkansas Mutual Insurance Company, a company financed by local men.

In the discharge of his duties in this company he attracted the attention of T. H. Hayes, capitalist of Memphis, who was operating one of the largest undertaking concerns of the race. Mr. McConico had combined in him all the qualities for which Mr. Hayes was looking, and was made business manager of Mr. Hayes' various enterprises.

During all this time he continued to be actively interested in the Mosaics and had become the close and confidential adviser of the National Grand Master, the lamented Alexander. He found time to get away from the business in Memphis and accompany Mr. Alexander on many of his trips in the interest of the Mosaics. This was during the period of expansion in the organization. The organization expanded so rapidly that new methods had to be introduced in conducting its business.

Profiting by the mistakes of other organizations, Mr. McConico saw that an imperative need of the Order was a system whereby a careful check could be kept on the various offices and where modern business methods would be applied. The organization had granted "State's Rights" to subordinate lodges and this made manifold increase in financial executives. Therefore at the National Grand Lodge meeting held in 1911 in Little Rock, he introduced a resolution creating the office of National Auditor. So well did he present his resolution, analyzing every purpose and intent involved, that the resolution was overwhelmingly adopted. By reason of his preparation and ability, he was offered the place and very reluctantly resigned his position in Memphis and came back to Little Rock devoting his entire time to the Order. While his duty is primarily connected with the work, naturally coming under the head of auditing, Mr. McConico has been active in everything that looks to the development of the Order.

There is no man connected with the Order
that is any better known than he.

Mr. McConico is a brilliant writer and an
eloquent speaker and his services are in constant demand from all sections of the country.

Within the Order he enjoys a high degree
of popularity, which in itself is significant
when it is remembered what his principal
duty is.

There are many cases of inefficiency in business administration and some cases of dishonesty, all of which come under his immediate jurisdiction. He approaches each with
perfect candor and searching detail and yet
with such a degree of sympathetic attitude,
that even in the case of adverse findings, the
accused regard him as a friend. He is exact
in requirements, but withal tactful. He has
earned the soubriquet of "Watchdog of the
Treasury," and through his careful attention
of every financial detail, he has not only
saved thousands of dollars to the Order, but
through sane approach and tactful handling,

has recovered thousands of dollars that might have been lost through relentless prosecution.

He has initiated many new measures for the good of the organization. He was one of the first to see the possibility of instituting the Adequate Rate Department and has been made director of this division. This department is less than a year old, but has developed into one of the most important arms of the service of the organization. We prefer to let him tell in his own words the work of this particular department, which will be found in subsequent chapters.

Mr. McConico is active in many local organizations. He served acceptably as president of the local branch of the N. A. A. C. P., and rendered invaluable aid in fighting through the courts the famous Elaine riot cases.

He is a member of several Greek fraternities. In May, 1916, his Alma-Mater conferred the honorary degree of Master of Arts upon him. So well did he deliver his thesis upon this occasion that he was invited the next year to deliver the commencement address.

DR. J. G. THORNTON, NATIONAL MEDICAL
EXAMINER

J. G. Thornton, A. M., M. D., National
Medical Examiner of the Mosaic Templars of
America, was born in the State of Missouri,
and in his early childhood was taken to the
State of Mississippi, where he was reared and
received his education.

He attended Eureka High School, Vicks-
burg, Miss., and Alcorn A. & M. West Side.
He also graduated from the State College for
Teachers, Holly Spring, Miss., received the
A. M. degree from Campbell College, Jackson,
Miss., and finished his medical course from
Meharry Medical College, Nashville, Tenn.,
1902. He supported and educated himself
in these schools by working at hotels during
these intervals between school terms. After
his graduation he taught in the public schools
of Mississippi and Arkansas, during the
spring and summer months to earn money to
carry him through the medical college. He
came to Little Rock, Ark., immediately after
graduating and began the practice of medicine.

DR. J. G. THORNTON

NATIONAL GRAND MEDICAL EXAMINER

He connected himself early with the Mosaic Templars of America, and has been a financial member ever since. The first National Grand Lodge that he attended was at Paducah, Ky., in 1908. Here he was appointed chairman of the committee on credentials.

The organization had no medical department; at this meeting he introduced a resolution providing for a medical department and it passed unanimously. He was elected director of that department and served until 1911, at which time he was succeeded by Dr. Darden of Alabama. He was appointed Past National Grand Master and served in that position until 1917. At the Grand Lodge that was held at Little Rock, 1917, he was again elected National Medical Director.

In the National Grand Lodge, 1921, he was re-elected. It was at this meeting that he brought forth the idea that the organization should have and operate hospitals for the benefit of its members, so that free treatment could be obtained at a minimum cost. He introduced a resolution to that effect. The National Grand Lodge passed favorably upon it but referred it to the States for approval. It was necessary for two-thirds of the States to approve it before it could become a law. All the States approved it save two. Dr. Thornton feels that this is one of the greatest efforts of his life, to make preparation to take care of all the afflicted members of this organization free of cost, except a small yearly assessment. The amount paid would hardly buy food for a sick member one day.

In speaking of the hospital idea Dr. Thornton said:

I believe the great Mosaic Templars of America should strive to be in a position to help alleviate the sufferings that will come to its membership through sickness, to be able to give them free treatment, nursing and housing is a great step forward, it shows that the organization has decided not to wait until you are dead to help you, by carrying you to a hospital and giving you the proper nursing and treatment from experienced and well prepared doctors and nurses. We are quite anxious to do all that we can for you while you live, and we believe you are going to join and make the hospital idea a success. We hope to train the women who are inclined to become trained nurses, in our own hospitals. This field offers quite an opportunity to our people, to become skilled in caring for the unfortunate members of the race. It also gives a profession that will bring handsome returns to those taking nurse training in a well regulated hospital. We hope to make these hospitals among the best in the country.

Dr. Thornton was married in 1904 to Miss Bessie Stephens. To them three children were born. Two are still living to bless their home. Miss Frances E. Thornton, who is a student in Wilbeforce University, and Florence Marjorie three years of age.

Mrs. C. E. Stephens, mother of Mrs. J. G. Thornton, is a teacher in the Gibbs High School in Little Rock, Ark. She has taught for fifty-five years in the public schools and at this time is teaching Latin and Science. Mrs. Stephens was called upon some years ago when the Mosaics first started out to prepare some of the literature for the organization. She assisted Mr. Bush on several occasions to prepare and arrange the same.

Dr. Thornton takes an active part in matters pertaining to the organization, also civic and political matters pertaining to his race. He never fails to perform a duty whenever an opportunity is given. He is now president of the Colored Chamber of Commerce, which has for its object to improve the conditions of the race, to promote business and professional relations among the business and professional men, also better schools for the race, to make conditions better around the home and to speak for them whenever their rights are being infringed. He served as chairman of the Defense Fund Commission, which raised more than $12,000.00 to see that justice was done to accused citizens, by due process of law, and the results were gratifying; twelve were accused, six went absolutely free and six got short terms in prison.

He does not believe in shielding criminals, but that they should have their day in court and be adjudged guilty or innocent by the court of the land and as citizens we all should stand for law and order.

He is a member of the Greek Fraternity in the city and was the first president. When the Elks were set up in this city a few months ago a committee of members called on Dr.

MRS. C. C. BELL

NATIONAL GRAND GUARDIAN

Thornton and insisted that he should be first Exalted Ruler. By much persuasion from some of his close friends he decided to take it.

He is also a trustee of his church and Shorter College, a member of the Knights of Pythias, Masonic Lodge, Odd Fellows, United Brother of Friendship, Good Samaritan, Court of Calanthe, and it goes without saying that he is a member of the Mosaic Templars of America. His first experience in secret organizations was in this Order, and he has always been a true Mosaic.

He has also seen the organization grow from three employees, until they now number into the hundreds.

MRS. C. C. BELL, NATIONAL GRAND GUARDIAN

It may be succinctly stated that the opportunity to serve humanity is the highest attainable honor. No one can foresee what destiny holds in store for them. When in the little hamlet of Antoine, Arkansas, a little girl first saw the light of day no one could look down the corridors of time and see that in the years to come this little tot would grow up to womanhood and the future destiny of a large per cent of the future men and women would be put in her keeping. Such is the story of the Grand Guardian of the Juvenile Department, Mrs. C. C. Bell.

Mrs. Bell's rise has been as spectacular as the fame of the county from which she came, Pike County, the only place in the United States producing diamonds.

In Mrs. Bell, Pike County has given the race a diamond no less real.

Coming to Little Rock in 1905 with her husband who had accepted a position as teacher in Williams Industrial Institute, she at once became identified with the organization and entered upon a career of service, paralleled by few women in the Order. So well did she do the humble duties given her that in 1910 she was elected State Aaronic Mistress of Arkansas, the only woman ever attaining this rank i nthe Order.

In 1911 she was elected the first State Grand Guardian of Arkansas. At this time there were only seven chartered Palaces in the State. Taking the initiative, she added in her first few months seventeen more Palaces. In this same year she was winner of the "$200.00 in gold" prize which was awarded to the "best worker" in the jurisdiction. When the Juvenile branch was made a National Department, she was elected to the head of same under title of National Grand Guardian and has been re-elected censecutively.

At the creation of the Juveniles into a National Department there were 600 children in the entire membership, while today, largely through her influence, the number reaches into the thousands.

The funds of the department at the time of her election were negligible; the latest audit of this department shows assets of $26,-851.06. To appreciate what this sum of money means, it is to be remembered that it was raised through a taxation of only eight and one-third cents per month.

The Juvenile Department is guarded with jealous care by all officials, for this is the training ground of the future Mosaics.

Mrs. Bell enjoys the confidence of the entire administrative force.

C. E. AND A. E. BUSH
(By. P. L. Dorman.)

The career and conduct of many of the young people of our race, who were born into superior advantages and inherited wealth from their parents, have in many cases, been deep disappointments to their friends. The acquisition of wealth, unearned by them, seems to affect their poise. Fortunes are quickly dissipated, and to use a common parlance they "run through what their folks leave them."

The Bush boys, as they are familiarly called in Little Rock, are notable exceptions. Their father was in splendid financial condition when they were small boys. They cannot claim, as so many must, that they ever experienced want or hardship. At the death of

C. E. BUSH

NATIONAL GRAND SCRIBE-TREASURER

their father, they came into the larger portion of his estate according to the expressed terms of his will. This did not change them in their general bearing, rather it seemed to impress them, that the public expected them to measure up to the standard set by their father.

Fortunately for them the father was spared to see his sons reach man's estate and took special pains to guide them along the lines that had been followed by him so successfully. Each one seems to have inherited the keen business tact of their father. They have shown a rare degree of "push and hustle" and through conservative investments have greatly increased the estate left them.

C. E. BUSH

C. E. Bush being the older of the sons, had thrust upon him the mantle of his father. When merely a youth, he was given responsible work to do in connection with the Order. He worked from the ground floor up. Being the son of Mr. Bush brought him no special favors. His father exacted from him the same service that he did from any employee. As

soon as he had proven himself worthy in the
humbler positions, he like the rest was promoted, merit alone being considered. When
official duties of his father became so heavy
that he could no longer edit the Guide, the
official publication, C. E. Bush was given
charge of same. As editor and manager of
the Guide he brought it to a high state of
efficiency. His administration of this office
was marked by great expansion in the mechanical department. Much new and modern
equipment was installed and the plant of the
Guide compared favorably with other plants
owned and operated by colored people. While
the operation of the Guide plant was never intended to produce revenue, C. E. Bush not
only made it self-sustaining but always carried
over a neat balance.

Many young people found employment in
the plant and in this the Mosaics again found
opportunity to render a real and practical
service to the race. When the Monument Departments of the several States were centralized this created a new central department

and it was necessary to find an experienced and capable head. The choice fell unanimously on C. E. Bush by reason of the splendid record he had made as manager of the Mosaic Guide printing plant. He continued in this service until called to the higher position of National Grand Scribe and Treasurer.

In both positions his administration was marked with an unusual degree of efficiency and business success. He kept each department up and abreast of modern methods in conduct and accounting.

In the midst of his busy career he was stricken with apoplexy—the result, according to his physicians, of overwork. From the time that he succeeded to his father's position in the Order, he became a slave to his work; day in and day out, he could be found on the job. His friends saw the strain under which he was laboring and entreated him to take a much-needed rest, but to no avail; he turned deaf ears to friends' and to his family doctor's entreaties and stuck to the job which has caused a sorrowful affliction.

Mr. Bush was a young man, full of promise for a brilliant future and his affliction has cast a gloom over his friends, who are legion. He is possessed of indomitable will power and is making a brave fight for the restoration of his health.

A. E. BUSH, ACTING NATIONAL GRAND SCRIBE
AND TREASURER

When C. E. Bush was stricken with an apoplectic stroke, it was apparent that for many months he would be incapacitated to discharge the duties of his office. There was only one person who had sufficient knowledge of the working of the great central department of the Endowment who could go immediately in and assume the reins of directing without a break; that man was A. E. Bush, the younger son of J. E. Bush.

The Executive Committee installed him at once in this important position and so well did he have a grasp of the situation that the machinery of this great department continued to function without a hitch. For three years he has served as Acting National Grand Scribe.

This is one of the most responsible positions in the gift of the Order and is worthy of the aspirations of any man. It is safe to say that there is not a young man of color, in the entire country, who is the responsible directing head of a business of such proportions, as he, as Acting National Grand Scribe and Treasurer. In his official capacity he is the custodian of assets in excess of one million dollars. It is difficult to the average mind to grasp the magnitude of a sum of more than one-half million dollars, and yet this is the vast sum of money passing through the hands of the National Grand Scribe and Treasurer each fiscal year. Not only is he charged with the receiving of this money, but he has the responsibility of disbursing the same, and in many cases, in the absence of specific law, he must use his own judgment in accepting or rejecting certain claims. This proves one of the most vexing problems in this department; notwithstanding the very binding obligation that each member takes on coming into the Order, there are many cases where members do not hesitate to take advantage of the Order by filing unworthy claims; some do this by design, others with wilful intent to defraud.

It is always an easy matter to secure sympathetic listeners, when a claim has been turned down and it is charged that the Order is beating members out of just claims. Mr. Bush has had wonderful success in satisfying such individuals. He is tactful, gives patient hearing to every complaint and usually strikes a happy medium of adjustment. There has never been an era in the history of the Order, when there was more general satisfaction than at the present time.

The success attending his administration, while marked by positive results, is a reasonable expectation. A. E. Bush was literally born into the Order, and from infancy, was the constant associate of his father, save for the years he was away from home attending school. Aside from completing the course of Gibbs High School, in his home city, he took a special course at Tuskegee Institute in Business Administration and leaving there he matriculated at Howard University. Upon returning home his father immediately took him into the Endowment Department as his private secretary. This position served as his apprenticeship, and he learned every detail of the work. When his father could no longer give personal attention to the office, by reason of failing health, the direction of the work fell directly upon him, although he had scarcely attained his majority in years.

He continued in this capacity until the death of his father, which created a vacancy that had to be permanently filled. In the minds of the Executive Committee the choice of successor would naturally come from one of the two sons of the founder. C. E. Bush was selected, the determining factor being his seniority, and A. E. Bush assumed the Secretary-Treasurer-ship of the Monument Department. He continued in this office until called upon to take charge of the Endowment Department, for reasons already mentioned.

Mr. Bush has impressed all as a clean-cut business man. No man in the city has a better standing with business men generally, than he has. Of a retiring disposition, and though giving close application to his business, Mr. Bush finds time for much personal attention to church and civic activities. He is a devoted member of the Congregational Church and holds the office of Treasurer. He is liberal to all good movements, and enjoys the confidence of the entire community as a young man of unimpeachable character.

THE REV. JOHN WASHINGTON GOODGAME, NATIONAL AARONIC GRAND MASTER

In the Rev. John W. Goodgame of Birmingham, Alabama, the Mosaic Templars have one of their shining examples of the modern day Christian minister, well prepared to lead his people, and who readily saw what a strong auxiliary a fraternity like the Mosaics, built on Christian foundations, would mean to his people in a moral and material way.

The Rev. Goodgame is one of the leading ministers of the Baptist faith and after his

REV. JNO. W. GOODGAME

NATIONAL AARONIC GRAND
MASTER

church there is nothing closer to his heart than
the cause of the Mosaic Templars. He became
connected with the organization in the early
days of its struggles, when it was rather difficult to get men of his type and influence interested in struggling fraternities. He was an experienced man, he saw the possibilities of such
an organization controlled by the proper type
of men; he put his shoulder to the wheel; became Grand Master Powell's right hand man;
today Alabama leads the jurisdiction.

The Rev. Goodgame started in life under
most adverse circumstances. Born on a farm,
he was a victim of all that a poor colored boy
usually received; plenty of labor without adequate reward. To many boys who did not
possess the Goodgame grit and ambition, the
case would have been hopeless. Amid all of
his toil and unfavorable environment he had
time for sober meditation. Two things he
determined to do—get an education and become a leader for his people. He failed in
neither. Without money, but with a determination to go through with it, he entered

Talladega College in 1885 and went through its several departments. While pursuing his theological course at Talladega he provided his means of support by pastoring the country churches in the vicinity of Talladega. He worked steadily upward and today is pastor of one of the leading churches in Birmingham, an edifice that was erected through his persistent efforts at a cost of $80,000.00 and will stand for the years that are to come as his monument.

Aside from his multi-fold duties as a minister and his active work as a fraternal man, Dr. Goodgame is associated with many business enterprises of the race.

In 1890 he was married to Miss Mary Bledsoe and to this happy union five children were born, and now all practically grown and well educated and are a credit to him and to the race.

COMMITTEE OF MANAGEMENT
MRS. ZENOBIA TRIMBLE

Mrs. Zenobia Trimble, Wichita Falls, Texas, member of the National Committee of Management, was one of the early members of the Order, when it was first planted in the "Empire State," Texas, joining in 1909. From that time up to now she has been on the firing line for Mosaic principle and prestige. Through her earnest and unselfish efforts and keen business insight shown through her work on committees in various National Grand meetings she was a unanimous choice for a place on the Committee of Management and has given her loyal service and hearty co-operation to this committee since 1914. Through her efforts the little Chamber with which she united, has grown from a membership of thirteen to eighty members and owns valuable city property in Wichita Falls.

MRS. JANIE WESTMORELAND BLAKELY

The watchword of the entire life and works of Janie Westmoreland Blakely has been service to the Mosaic Templars of America. Her record has been one of tried and proved efficiency of a woman who delights in rendering real service to the Order. Her ripe experience, mature judgment, unquestioned integrity and ability have been sources of pride to her friends and of profit to the Order.

In 1892 she connected herself with the Mosaic Templars of America, under Mrs. Eva McIntosh in the Juvenile Department. In 1893 she was elected as a Juvenile delegate to the National Grand Lodge which convened in Little Rock, Ark., in the Thompson Hall. In 1896 she was elected National Committeewoman, since that time she has served on the National Committee with honors. She has organized many lodges and added hundreds of members to the Order, served as Secretary from time to time at the National Grand Lodges.

When the Order was in its infancy and unable to defray her expenses to the different State Grand Lodges she defrayed her own expenses and has never missed but one Grand Lodge during the twenty-eight years of her

GROUP OF MEMBERS OF NATIONAL COMMITTEE OF MANAGEMENT
1. Mrs. Eva Green Cannon, Ohio
2. Mrs. Zenobia Trimble, Texas
3. Mrs. Janie W. Blakely, Ill.
4. Mrs. Mattie L. Griffin, Okla.
5. Mrs. Mary L. McCoy, Ala.
6. Mrs. L. G. Shanklin, Ark.

service in the Mosaic Templars of America.
Mrs. Janie Westmoreland Blakely is still at
her post.

MRS. L. G. SHANKLIN

Mrs. L. G. Shanklin is the only woman
from Arkansas on the National Committee of
Management. She is a resident of the progressive town of Fordyce, Ark., and has the distinction of presiding over one of the largest
Chambers in the jurisdiction of Arkansas.
She is easily the outstanding woman of her
community and heads every forward movement in church or social affairs.

She has been a member of the Order for sixteen years and has been one of its faithful
workers. In recognition of her splendid work
she was elevated to her present high position
and for the past three years that she has served
as a member of the Committee of Management has made a most favorable impression
on the associate members as a woman of calm
and deliberate judgment, congenial and dependable. All of Arkansas, the mother State,
feel honored through her.

MRS. EVA GREEN CANNON

Mrs. Eva Green Cannon is the type of woman who is making her influence felt in the big affairs of the race. She is one of the dominant figures on the Committee of Management. She is cultured and possesses a pleasing personality. For a number of years she was one of the prominent teachers in the city schools of Nashville.

The Mosaic work has had her unselfish support particularly in her State, Tennessee. Much of the prestige which the Order enjoys in that State is directly due to her influence.

She was a commanding figure in church, civic and social affairs in Nashville, prior to her removal to Cleveland, Ohio, where she now resides. Hundreds of young people acclaim her as their guardian angel.

MRS. MATTIE L. GRIFFIN

Since 1921 Mrs. Mattie Griffin has been a most valuable member to the Committee of Management. She has had superior advantages and is possessed of a classical education.

She is the wife of a prominent and successful physician of Oklahoma. For years she has stood in the front ranks of the teaching profession in that State. She is active in every movement for the uplift of her people.

Mrs. Griffin worked from the ranks up to her present position in the Order. She was the first State Grand Scribe for the jurisdiction of Oklahoma, and consequently served as State Burial Secretary and Secretary of the Temple Board.

MRS. MARY L. M'COY

A woman of ability and untiring devotion to the Mosaic organization. She exemplifies in her activities on the Committee of Management, qualities of mind and heart which so generally characterize her sex. She became a member of the Order in 1900 and was made presiding officer of the Chamber of which she was a charter member. She has been continuously elected as the Zephro Mistress. Through her zeal and success in spreading the Mosaic cause in the great industrial center, Birmingham, Ala., she was picked for promotion, the opportunity came and in 1916 Dr. S. J. Elliott appointed her a member of the National Committee of Management.

TWO PIONEER GRAND MASTERS

P. H. JORDAN, STATE GRAND MASTER OF ARKANSAS

It would be hard to find a man in the entire jurisdiction, who possesses a higher degree of qualities that go to make an ideal leader of men. Possessed of commanding physique and striking personality; having an abundance of wholesome information, gained from an active life, dating from boyhood, void of conceit, courteous to all, sympathetic in attitude, he has built himself securely in the hearts of the people of Arkansas.

Mr. Jordan became a Mosaic in 1899 and although he was among the youngest of the group, he soon attracted recognition of the older heads. Mr. Jordan always had the courage of his convictions and often threw

P. H. JORDAN
S. G. M. OF ARKANSAS

L. L. POWELL
S. G. M. OF ALABAMA

dismay into the ranks of the older and ultra-conservative officials.

As touched upon elsewhere, he was the father of the "State Rights" idea which was an unpopular idea to the older heads, who subscribed to the theory, "Old men for counsel—young men for war." But Mr. Jordan belonged to that group of young men who had vision and the success of several new features that he was instrumental in fathering, has justified the wisdom of his contentions.

Aside from championing the creation of State jurisdictions, he was the able assistant of L. L. Powell, who conceived the idea of the Grand Masters' Council, which has developed into a kind of clearing house of Mosaic policy and activity. He served for several years as President of the Council and refused re-election at the last sitting of the Council in 1923. He was succeeded by L. L. Powell, Grand Master of Alabama.

The crowning triumph of his long career as State Grand Master was the erection of the beautiful and commodious State Temple

Building, in Little Rock, at a cost in excess of $100,000.00 for erection and furnishing. Mr. Jordan is one of the most popular Grand Masters in the entire jurisdiction and the idol of the Mosaics of Arkansas.

When he became Grand Master in 1906, there were only forty-three lodges in the State having a combined membership of six hundred. During his continued administration these lodges have increased to 905, with a membership that once reached to 30,000. Mr. Jordan was born in the State of Mississippi, and by reason of the large family which his parents had, he had to leave school quite early and is largely a graduate from the university of experience.

He has been thrifty and frugal. He was blessed with a family of ten, eight of whom are living, to whom he has been able to give every educational advantage. His first wife, Mrs. Annie Flora Jordan, a most lovable character, died in 1918, and in 1920 he was married to Miss Lena Lowe, an accomplished lady of Cordelle, Ga.

Today Alabama has over 500 organized lodges with a membership of more than 30,000.

For twenty-three years Mr. Powell has been one of the leading figures in making Mosaic history.

In carrying the Order to the heights reached in Alabama, Grand Master Powell has a system peculiarly his own. In his peculiar way, he has made himself the dominant figure in his State. The entire membership has full confidence in him and yield him its full cooperation.

One of the notable achivements of Grand Master Powell was the creation of the Grand Masters' Council. He was the father of this idea and was ably assisted by his co-worker, P. H. Jordan. The Grand Masters' Council has been one of the powerful adjuncts of the organization. It has no authority to legislate, but acts in an advisory capacity. The membership is restricted to the Grand Masters of the several States, but membership is not com-

L. L. POWELL, STATE GRAND MASTER
OF ALABAMA

L. L. Powell, as State Grand Master of Alabama, enjoys the distinction of being the head of the largest jurisdiction of the Order. For years Arkansas, the Mother State, had this distinction, but Alabama is a far more populous State than Arkansas, and Powell has had a much larger field from which to draw.

Mr. Powell was born near Conyers, Ga., October, 1876, and was educated in the schools of Atlanta. Leaving Georgia, he decided to locate in Alabama in the little city of Sheffield. Here he entered the mercantile business and was successful from the start. His business ability as a young man attracted the attention of the National officials in their quest of the proper type of man to bring order out of the chaotic conditions existing in Alabama. In the meeting of the State Grand Lodge in 1909 at Opelika, Ala., he was chosen State Grand Master. At the time of his selection there were only 43 lodges in the State, with an approximate membership of 2,000.

MRS. JENNIE M. MILLER
S. G. S. OF ARKANSAS

MRS. AMANDA DAVIS
S. G. S. OF ALABAMA

pulsory. At present he is President of the Council.

The National officials have the utmost confidence in Grand Masters Jordan and Powell and by reason of their long active connection with the Order in official capacity their views are often sought in weighty matters with which the chief officials must deal. They are the deans of the entire jurisdicion and are held in esteem and veneration by all the Associate Grand Masters.

TWO SENIOR STATE GRAND SCRIBES

The office of Grand Scribe is the keystone of the successful administration of any Grand Master. For a State jurisdiction to continue to function in all its parts, no one enters into this possibility more than the Grand Scribe. This officer must enter into the closest official relations with the Grand Master, and if he is to succeed the Grand Scribe must be loyal, trustworthy, efficient and scrupulously honest.

The Mosaic Templars have from the beginning conceded to woman equal shares in all of the work of the Order. In keeping this balance it has become an unwritten law that the position of State Grand Scribe shall go to some worthy and efficient woman. All of the State Grand Scribes have as a rule been women of exceptional ability and have reflected credit on the high place to which they have been elevated.

Two types, by reason of their long service, have been selected for a place in this volume, and for the reasons that they too are pioneers in the work and are the Scribes of the jurisdictions that are presided over by the two Grand Masters whose short biographies have been given.

MRS. JENNIE M'COY MILLER

Mrs. Jennie McCoy Miller is a native of Georgia. She was brought from Macon by her father when she was quite young. Mrs. Miller is the product of the Little Rock Public Schools, being a graduate of the old Union High School, which is now known as Gibbs High School.

There is no woman who has been continuously connected in an official way with the Order as long as she has been. The Founders of the Order were in need of a woman of the type of Mrs. Miller and succeeded in interesting her in the work back in the days of its struggle for existence. She accepted the offer, largely out of pride for home, city and State, and from the day she came into the organization to the present time she has been a faithful worker. In point of service she is the oldest Grand Scribe in the Order. She was elected to this position at the session held in Hot Springs, 1907, and has been re-elected each time, in most cases without an opponent. She is conceded to be one of the most efficient officials in the Order.

Although she is a most loyal and uncompromising member of the Mosaics, she is an active member in other fraternities and has held many offices of honor and trust in them.

She is a vital force in civic organizations and through her club activities she has done much for the suffering and needy of her race.

As a church member she is one of its most dependable members.

Mrs. Miller is truly a woman that reflects credit on her race.

MRS. AMANDA DAVIS, STATE GRAND SCRIBE, ALABAMA

Mrs. Davis' service as State Grand Scribe of Jurisdiction of Alabama is co-equal with that of Grand Master Powell. To speak of Mosaic Templars in Alabama is to speak of Mrs. Davis. As a State Grand Scribe she has endeared herself to the Mosaics of Alabama to the same degree as her Grand Master. They are a complete example of a team working in harmony for the good of all. In the long years that they have served it is not recorded that there has ever been friction beween them or the least suspicion of jealousy.

The National Auditor never fails, in mentioning efficient officers, to include the name of Mrs. Amanda Davis. With all the success that has come to her in an official way she is the same simple, unobtrusive, willing servant of the people who delight to honor her.

Grand Master Powell, in speaking of the admirable traits of Mrs. Davis said there was no more valuable subordinate in the entire jurisdiction. One to whom you can delegate a certain mission to perform or a certain piece of work to do, and then forget it, confident that when it comes next to your attention that it will come in the form of a report that the thing has been well done.

It is peculiarly fitting that the mission of this humble little volume should conclude with a complimentary sketch of one so well deserving of praise at the hands of all Mosaics.